Remember When People Used to Boast About Having "Chicken Every Sunday"?

Now you can afford to have chicken every day of the week; it's one of the best meat buys on the market. And it's loaded with proteins, low in calories, easily digested. It's oh-so-tasty, too.

If you want all the good things chicken can give you, but you want variety as well, here are many ways to prepare this delicious food. Boiled, fried, baked; in main dishes, soups, sandwiches, salads; as a meal-in-a-minute or an elaborate gourmet treat.

Here are almost two hundred recipes covering the whole range of chicken cookery. With this book, you can have chicken seven days a week—in a different, delectable way every time.

THE SUPER CHICKEN COOKBOOK

IONA NIXON

Contents

I	An Introduction to Chicken	9
II	Fried Chicken	11
III	Broiling Chicken	19
IV	Roast Chicken	31
V	Chicken Soups	47
VI	Chicken Sandwiches	61
VII	International Chicken Recipes	72
VIII	Chicken in a Hurry	92
IX	Chicken Salads	111
X	Chicken Oriental	121
XI	Chicken Casseroles	136
XII	Stewing Chicken	151
XIII	Chicken for the Gourmet	161
	Index	173

THE
SUPER
CHICKEN
COOKBOOK

Chapter I

AN INTRODUCTION TO CHICKEN

BARELY A GENERATION ago, chicken was so scarce and expensive it was strictly reserved for Sunday dinner. The seasons determined what kind of chicken you were to have at that dinner, too. In the spring only broilers and fryers were available. In summer you could find heavier fryers, and in the fall you could buy roasting hens or stewing chickens. Today, thanks to American know-how, all that has changed.

The American housewife can have any kind of chicken she wants, at any time of the year, at a fraction of what it used to cost. To most of our parents, chicken was considered an expensive food. Today, thanks to improved farming and production methods, chicken has turned out to be the best meat buy on the market, cheaper than beef, pork, lamb or veal. As for food value, it is loaded with easily assimilated proteins; and chicken is perhaps the most easily digestible food there is. It is excellent fare for young and old alike, the most adaptable meat on the market.

Broilers or fryers, stewing chicken, roasting chicken or chicken parts are all readily available in your modern supermarket. Chickens can be bought ready to cook, frozen or canned. If your family loves drumsticks, you can buy drumsticks only. If their fancy runs to chicken breasts, you can buy them only, too.

Capons, male chickens with sex privileges removed, are readily available. Their white meat portion is more generous than that on the average chicken; their weight is usually in the four-to-six-pound category. They are ideal for roasting or stewing.

Cornish hens have been plentiful on the market in recent years; these are a delight to serve. Their weight is around a pound and their flavor would make an epicurean flip.

Fresh chicken will keep in the refrigerator approximately two days. Frozen chicken, properly wrapped, will keep indefinitely in the freezer. When fresh chicken is stored in the refrigerator it should not be tightly wrapped. In fact, both ends of the package should be left open, and the package should be placed in the coldest part of the refrigerator. Be sure to remove the gizzard, liver and heart packet; put this in a separate covered dish.

Packaged frozen chicken will thaw if placed in the refrigerator overnight. To thaw frozen chicken *quickly,* place it, wrappings and all, under running water until the joints can be flexed. Frozen chicken pies can be popped into the oven right from the freezer.

Canned chicken may be an excellent buy or it may turn out to be very expensive. A can of boned chicken is fine when you need just a small amount of canapés or small sandwiches. But as a meal for a family of four or more, canned boned chicken will hardly make a dent in the appetites unless you provide a separate can for each one.

Whole canned chicken is also available. This is ideal when you are in a rush, or to keep on your "unexpected company" shelf. This chicken is usually very tender, due to the steam process of canning. Since chicken in the can is not graded as salmon or tuna fish are, always purchase a brand you know is reliable. If you come across a bargain in whole canned chicken, be sure to check for the government inspection label. I usually shun bargains in canned chicken with unknown brand names; there's many a scrawny bird hiding inside.

Nowadays chicken is truly a universal food. It is a great favorite in the Orient and in Europe, Mexico and South America as well as in the United States. Killing the fattest hen in the barnyard for a special-occasion dinner is indeed a thing of the past. Now we can have chicken every day at a fraction of what it used to cost our parents. The old political promise of a chicken in every pot has definitely come true!

Chapter II

FRIED CHICKEN

CHICKEN IS A delicately flavored, tender meat, but it lends itself well to frying; it is one of the few meats that does not completely change character and flavor when it is fried. Though frying in the true sense of the word means to cook in deep fat, in the case of chicken cookery we are using sautéing to mean frying, too.

When selecting a chicken for frying, always watch the package label carefully. The label should read "broiler" or "fryer." If you inadvertently get a stewing hen, no amount of frying will turn it into a very palatable dish.

Broilers or fryers are usually tender enough to need only 30 to 40 minutes of cooking. They should never be overdone, for then you get too much of the fried taste and not enough of the delicate chicken flavor.

Broilers or fryers can be skillet fried, French fried or oven fried. You will find recipes for all of these methods in this chapter.

PRETZEL FRIED CHICKEN

2 2- to 3-pound fryer-broilers, cut up into portion-sized pieces
2 eggs, beaten until lemon yellow
½ cup milk
3 cups finely crushed pretzel crumbs made from the cocktail type pretzels
Vegetable oil or shortening for deep frying

Dry the pieces of chicken with paper toweling. Mix the eggs and milk thoroughly.

Place the finely crushed pretzels in a paper sack. Dip each piece of chicken in the egg-milk mixture; then place in the crushed pretzels and shake sack until thoroughly coated.

Drop into 350° vegetable oil and fry until a rich golden brown. Place the fried pieces of chicken on aluminum foil in a large flat baking pan in a 300° F. oven for an additional 35 minutes. Serve piping hot. Serves 6.

BUTTERMILK FRIED CHICKEN

2 fryers, approximately 1½ pounds each
2 cups all-purpose flour
1½ teaspoons baking powder
1½ teaspoons baking soda
½ teaspoon salt
¼ teaspoon pepper
3 cups buttermilk
Fat for deep frying

Cut the chicken into serving pieces. Put the flour in a paper sack, then place two pieces of chicken at a time in the flour; shake well so that they are completely covered.

Add the baking powder, baking soda, salt and pepper to the flour that is left in the sack. Shake well to be sure all is well mixed.

Dip each piece of chicken in the buttermilk, then place it in the flour mixture in the sack. Shake well so that the chicken is completely covered with the flour mixture.

Drop the pieces of floured chicken into 350° F. hot fat. Fry until golden brown. If you do not have an automatic electric French fryer, use a hot-fat thermometer. It is important that you fry the chicken until it is thoroughly done. If you are not sure, you can complete cooking by placing the fried pieces of chicken on a rack in a 350° F. oven for an additional 15 or 20 minutes. Serve piping hot. Serves 4.

MARYLAND FRIED CHICKEN

2 2- to 3-pound fryer- broilers, cut up into portion-sized pieces
1 teaspoon salt
½ teaspoon pepper
1 teaspoon Accent
1 cup fine dry bread crumbs
2 eggs, beaten until lemon yellow
2 tablespoons half and half cream
¼ pound butter

For the gravy:

3 tablespoons all-purpose flour
½ teaspoon salt
¼ teaspoon pepper
1½ cups half and half cream

Wipe the pieces of chicken with paper toweling. Mix the salt, pepper, Accent and bread crumbs thoroughly. Mix the eggs and the 2 tablespoons of half and half cream. Dip each piece of chicken into the egg-cream mixture and then into the bread crumbs. Be sure that each piece is thoroughly coated.

Melt the butter in a large skillet and sauté each piece of chicken until it is well browned on all sides. Turn the heat down to very low and continue to cook for 1 hour, or until the thickest portions of the chicken can be pierced with a fork.

Place the chicken on a hot platter in a 250° F. oven while you are making the gravy. To the butter left in the skillet, add flour, salt and pepper; cook over low heat until it is bubbly and the flour begins to brown slightly. Stir in the cream and cook over very low heat, stirring constantly, until the mixture is thickened. Pour over the hot chicken and serve at once. Serves 6.

GARLIC FLAVORED FRIED CHICKEN

2 2- to 3-pound fryer-broilers, cut up into portion-sized pieces
¾ cup milk
4 cloves of garlic, minced
½ teaspoon Accent
3 eggs, beaten until lemon yellow
1 cup all-purpose flour
½ teaspoon garlic powder
½ teaspoon salt
¼ teaspoon pepper
2 cups fine bread crumbs
Vegetable oil for deep frying

Wipe the chicken pieces with paper toweling. Mix the milk, garlic and Accent and let stand for a few minutes for flavors to unite. Add the eggs to the milk. Put each piece of chicken in a paper sack with the flour and coat the chicken by shaking thoroughly.

Mix the garlic powder, salt and pepper with the bread crumbs. Dip the chicken into the eggs and milk and then into the flavored bread crumbs. Drop into 350° F. hot oil and fry until a rich golden brown.

Place the browned chicken on a rack in a 350° F. oven for an additional 30 minutes. Serve at once, piping hot. Serves 6.

HUSH-PUPPY FRIED CHICKEN

2 2- to 3-pound fryers, cut up into portion-sized pieces
½ cup all-purpose flour
½ cup yellow corn meal
½ teaspoon salt
¼ teaspoon pepper
2 cups buttermilk
2 cups hush-puppy mix (onion-flavored variety)
Vegetable oil for deep frying

Mix the flour and corn meal together in a paper sack. Place each piece of chicken in the sack and shake thoroughly to coat completely.

Mix the salt, pepper and buttermilk together. Place the hush-puppy mix in another paper sack. Dip each piece of chicken in the seasoned buttermilk and then drop it into the hush-puppy mix and shake to coat thoroughly.

Heat vegetable oil to 350° F. and drop each piece of coated chicken into it. Fry until a rich golden brown. Place in a flat baking dish and place in a 325° F. oven for an additional 30 minutes. Serve at once, piping hot. Serves 6.

Note: If you cannot obtain hush-puppy prepared mix in your store, substitute the following: 2 cups white corn meal, 2 teaspoons baking powder, 1 teaspoon onion powder, ½ teaspoon salt, 4 tablespoons butter. Work all together until it is of a fine consistency and then use as the breading mixture as specified in the above recipe. I use hush-puppy prepared mix because it is a timesaving shortcut.

FRIED CHICKEN WITH PINEAPPLE AND TOMATOES

2 fryers or broilers, approximately 1½ pounds each
¾ cup all-purpose flour
½ teaspoon salt
¼ teaspoon pepper
1 teaspoon paprika
8 tablespoons butter
1 13½-ounce can pineapple chunks, juice and all
3 medium-sized tomatoes

Cut the chicken into serving pieces. Place the flour, salt, pepper and paprika in a paper sack. Shake several times to mix well. Place two or three pieces of chicken at a time in the flour sack, and shake well so that the chicken is completely coated.

Melt the butter in a large skillet and arrange the pieces of chicken over the bottom so they will all brown evenly. Cook over moderate heat until the chicken is a rich golden brown. Turn the pieces frequently to assure even browning.

Add the pineapple chunks and juice to the chicken. Remove the stem portion of the tomatoes, cut them into wedges and arrange them in the pan with the chicken. Cover tightly and continue to cook over moderate heat for 35 minutes. Remove the cover and cook for 10 minutes longer, to reduce the liquid and to crisp the chicken. Place chicken on a heated platter and pour any remaining gravy over it. Serves 4.

FRIED CHICKEN AMANDINE

2 fryers or broilers, approximately 1½ pounds each
¾ cup all-purpose flour
½ teaspoon salt
¼ teaspoon pepper
1 teaspoon paprika
8 tablespoons butter
1 cup half and half cream
¾ cup blanched, slivered almonds
2 tablespoons chopped parsley

Cut up the chicken into serving pieces. Place the flour, salt, pepper and paprika in a paper sack. Shake several times to mix well. Place two pieces of chicken at a time in the flour sack and shake until the chicken is thoroughly coated.

Melt the butter in a large skillet and arrange the pieces of chicken so that they will fry evenly. Fry over moderate heat until the chicken is browned on both sides. Turn frequently to assure even browning. Turn the heat down to simmer, cover pan and continue to cook for 15 minutes longer.

After this 15-minute cooking period, add the cream; stir well, so that it is evenly distributed. Continue to cook over low heat for 15 minutes longer. Add the slivered almonds and cook for an additional 5 minutes. Place the chicken on a heated platter, pouring the cream and almonds over it. Garnish with the chopped parsley. Serves 4.

SIMPLE OVEN FRIED CHICKEN

1 3-pound fryer-broiler, cut into portion-sized pieces
½ pound margarine
½ teaspoon salt
¼ teaspoon pepper
2 cups fine bread crumbs
2 tablespoons cornstarch

Wipe the pieces of chicken with paper toweling.

Melt the margarine in a saucepan. Mix the salt, pepper, bread crumbs and cornstarch together thoroughly. Dip each piece of chicken into the melted margarine and then into the bread crumb mixture. Place the chicken pieces, skin side down, in a shallow baking pan. Bake in a 350° F. oven for 45 minutes. Then turn each piece of chicken over, skin side up, and continue to bake at 350° F. for 25 minutes longer, or until a rich brown and each piece can be easily pierced with a fork. Serve at once, piping hot. Serves 4.

OVEN-FRIED CHICKEN #1

2 fryers, approximately 1½ pounds each
¾ cup all-purpose flour
½ cup corn meal
½ teaspoon salt
¼ teaspoon pepper
1 teaspoon paprika
½ cup melted butter

Cut the chicken into serving pieces. Place the flour, corn meal, salt, pepper and paprika in a paper sack. Shake several times so that all is well mixed.

Place two pieces of chicken in the flour sack at a time. Shake so that all the chicken is well coated.

Put the melted butter in the bottom of a baking dish big enough to accommodate all of the chicken pieces. Arrange the chicken in the baking dish, and place in a 350° F. oven for 1 hour. Turn the chicken several times during the baking time to assure even browning. Serves 4.

OVEN-FRIED CHICKEN #2

2 2- to 3-pound fryer-broilers, cut up into portion-sized pieces
1 cup buttermilk
1 teaspoon salt
¼ teaspoon pepper
5 cups corn flakes, crushed finely
2 tablespoons melted butter or margarine

Dry the chicken with paper toweling. Mix the buttermilk, salt and pepper together thoroughly. Using a pastry brush, coat each piece of chicken with the seasoned buttermilk.

Put the crushed corn flakes in a paper sack. Place the pieces of buttermilk-coated chicken in the corn flakes one at a time and shake well so they are thoroughly coated.

Spread the melted butter over the bottom of a pan large enough to accommodate all of the pieces of chicken laying flat. Put the corn flake-covered pieces of chicken in the melted butter, skin side up. Place in a 350° F. oven for 1 hour, or until the thickest portions of the chicken can be pierced with a fork and it is a rich golden brown. Serve piping hot. Serves 6.

Variations:
Use strained cream of celery soup instead of buttermilk.
Use strained cream of mushroom soup instead of buttermilk.
Use dairy sour cream instead of buttermilk.
Use two eggs, beaten until lemon yellow, and ¾ cup of milk instead of buttermilk.
Use crushed Wheaties instead of corn flakes and reduce heat to 325° F.
Use crushed Rice Crispies instead of corn flakes.

SIMPLE FRIED CHICKEN

2 fryers or broilers, approximately 1½ pounds each
6 tablespoons butter or margarine
½ teaspoon salt
¼ teaspoon pepper
½ teaspoon paprika
1 teaspoon Accent
½ teaspoon garlic salt (optional)

Cut the chicken into serving portions. Dry each piece well with paper toweling. Melt the butter in a large skillet. Place the chicken pieces in the skillet and fry slowly until they are evenly browned on both sides.

Sprinkle the salt, pepper, paprika, Accent and garlic salt over the chicken and cover the pan. Continue to cook over low heat for 35 minutes. During this cooking period, turn the pieces of chicken frequently to assure even distribution of the seasonings.

If you like your fried chicken crisp, remove the cover 10 minutes before serving. Turn each piece at least once. Garnish with chopped parsley if you desire additional color. Serves 4.

SKILLET FRIED CHICKEN

2 2-pound fryer-broilers, cut up into portion-sized pieces
1½ cups all-purpose flour
2 eggs, beaten until lemon yellow
1 cup milk
½ teaspoon salt
¼ teaspoon pepper
½ cup corn oil

Dry the chicken pieces with paper toweling. Sprinkle lightly with a small portion of the flour. Set aside.

Mix the eggs and milk together. Add the salt and pepper. Dip each piece of chicken into the egg-milk mixture and then into the flour, coating well on all sides.

Heat the corn oil in a large skillet; brown the chicken evenly on all sides. Turn the heat down to very low, cover and cook for another 30 minutes, or until the thickest pieces of chicken can be pierced with a fork. Serve at once, piping hot. Serves 4.

Chapter III
BROILING CHICKEN

BROILERS (OR FRYERS, as they are often called) are indeed in a class by themselves. There are many ways to cook them; you do not have to do it next to an open flame just because they are labeled broilers. There are many other methods of preparing them.

It takes a little bit of planning to make enough broiler chicken to go around, but the rewards in flavor are great. The weight range of broilers or fryers is usually from 1½ to 3 pounds dressed. I usually allow 1½ pounds of chicken for every two people. If you have ravenous appetites in your family you might have to figure on more.

Since these birds are young and tender, great care has to be taken not to overcook them and lose the delicate, young-chicken flavor. On the other hand, they have to be done well enough so there is never any oozing blood around the joints and the meat falls away from the bone with ease. Avoid jabbing with a fork frequently to test for doneness, as this provides an easy escape for all the good juices with which a broiler is blessed.

If you are putting broilers under a flame or into a hot oven, always put them skin side down in the pan first. This prevents the skin from shrinking away and the meat from drying out. Cooking with the skin side up last will give that pretty-as-a-picture look to your chicken when it is served. Since the skin on a broiler is tender and full of flavor, it is important to preserve it as much as possible.

If you are broiling chicken and it is not browning to your complete satisfaction, sprinkle a little paprika over it. There is something magic about chicken and paprika—the two just seem to unite to make an appetizingly browned appearance.

Due to their tenderness, broilers are wonderful for hurry-up meals. You can prepare a feast fit for a king while your guests are still on their first cocktail.

SIMPLE BARBECUED BROILERS

2 2-pound broilers, cut in half lengthwise
1 cup mayonnaise
2 tablespoons honey
2 tablespoons onion, chopped fine
1 teaspoon paprika
¼ teaspoon pepper
½ teaspoon salt

Mix the mayonnaise, honey, onion, paprika, pepper and salt together and let stand at room temperature for 30 minutes.

Using a pastry brush, coat each broiler inside and out with the flavored mayonnaise.

Place the broilers skin side down on the rack of the broiler about 10 inches away from the heat. Baste frequently during the first 20 minutes of broiling. Turn the chicken over, breast side up, and continue to broil and baste for an additional 25 minutes, or until the thickest part of the chicken can be pierced with a fork and it is golden brown.

OVEN BARBECUED BROILERS #1

2 2-pound broilers, cut in half lengthwise
1 cup wine vinegar
¾ cup peanut oil
2 eggs, beaten until lemon yellow
1 teaspoon salt
¼ teaspoon pepper
½ teaspoon pulverized sage
¼ teaspoon savory
¼ teaspoon thyme
1 teaspoon paprika
1 teaspoon brown sugar

Place the broiler halves in a mixture of the vinegar and oil about 45 minutes before you intend to start cooking them. Then remove and drain well. Save the vinegar and oil.

Add the vinegar and oil to the beaten eggs a little at a time and continue to beat with a rotary beater. Add the salt, pepper, sage, savory, thyme, paprika and brown sugar. Continue to beat until frothy.

Place the broiler halves, skin side down, on a broiling rack and pan about 10 inches from the heat. Baste them with the egg, vinegar and oil mixture every few minutes. After 20 minutes of broiling, turn the chicken over so that it is skin side up. Continue to broil and baste for another 30 minutes, or until the thickest portion of the breast can be pierced with a sharp fork.

This chicken can also be made over an outdoor charcoal fire or on a rotisserie. Serves 4.

BARBECUED BROILERS #2

2 broilers, 2 pounds each, cut into quarters
¼ cup melted butter
½ cup onion, chopped fine
¼ cup lemon juice
½ teaspoon grated lemon rind
2 cloves garlic, chopped fine
½ teaspoon salt
½ teaspoon celery seed
½ teaspoon dill seed
½ teaspoon chili powder
1 cup chili sauce
½ cup orange juice
¼ cup brown sugar
¼ cup cider vinegar

Melt the butter in a saucepan and add the onion; sauté until the onion is limp and tender. Stir in the lemon juice, lemon rind, garlic, salt, celery seed, dill seed and chili powder. Add the chili sauce, orange juice, brown sugar and cider vinegar. Cook over low heat for 15 minutes; stir frequently during cooking.

Brush the chickens inside and out with the sauce. Place on a broiler rack about 10 inches from the heat and continue to broil and baste for 15 minutes. Turn the pieces of chicken over every 15 minutes and continue to broil and baste until the thickest portions can be pierced with a fork.

This chicken can also be made over a charcoal fire or on a rotisserie. Slow cooking and frequent basting is the secret of its success. Serves 4.

OVEN BARBECUED BROILERS #3

2 2-pound broilers, cut in half lengthwise
3 tablespoons all-purpose flour
1 tablespoon powdered mustard
2 cups unsweetened pineapple juice
1 cup chili sauce
¼ cup onion, chopped fine
½ teaspoon salt
¼ teaspoon pepper
2 drops Tabasco (optional—if you like it hot)

Mix the flour, mustard and pineapple juice together. Add the chili sauce and onion; add the salt, pepper and Tabasco.

Place the broiler halves skin side down in a flat roasting pan. Pour the pineapple juice mixture over them and cover with aluminum foil. Bake in a 350° F. oven for 35 minutes.

Then turn the chicken over, breast side up, and continue to cook at 350° F. for another 25 minutes. Five minutes before serving, place under the broiler to allow the chicken to get crispy brown. Serve at once, piping hot. Serves 4.

BARBECUED BROILERS #4

3 2- to 3-pound broilers, cut in half lengthwise
1½ teaspoons salt
1 teaspoon Accent
¼ cup fresh lemon juice
1 cup granulated sugar
½ cup Worcestershire sauce
1 teaspoon seasoned pepper (found in the spice section of most stores)
¼ teaspoon cayenne (less if you do not like it hot)
¼ pound butter
½ cup grape brandy
1 cup tarragon wine vinegar

Mix the salt and Accent together. Sprinkle a bit of the mixture inside the ribcage; rub the remainder on the outside of the chicken. Set them aside while you make the sauce.

Place the rest of the ingredients in a saucepan over low heat. Stir frequently and cook until the sugar and butter have both melted. Always keep mixture just below boiling. Remove from the heat.

Place the chicken halves, breast side down, in a shallow pan in a 350° F. oven for 10 minutes. After this first 10 minutes, start basting the chicken at frequent intervals. After 30 minutes, turn the chicken over, breast side up. Continue to baste at frequent intervals. Roast for another 45 minutes, or until a fork will pierce the thickest portion with ease. Serve piping hot. Serves 6.

If you have any of the basting sauce left over, it can be stored for a week in the refrigerator.

BARBECUED BROILERS #5

4 2- to 3-pound broilers, cut in half lengthwise
2 teaspoons salt
1 teaspoon Accent
½ cup melted butter
1 teaspoon paprika
¾ cup lemon juice
½ teaspoon black pepper
2 tablespoons Heinz 57 steak sauce
¼ pound butter
1¼ cups apple cider vinegar

Sprinkle some of the salt and the Accent in the ribcage of the chickens. Rub the remainder of the salt on the outside. Put the chickens aside at least 20 minutes to permit the salt to melt in. Then brush the legs and breast of each chicken with the melted butter and place them breast side down in a shallow baking pan. Put them in a 400° F. oven for 15 minutes. Then turn the chickens over, breast side up, and cook at 400° F. for an additional 25 minutes, or until they begin to get golden brown.

While the chicken is roasting, place the paprika, lemon juice, pepper, steak sauce, butter and cider vinegar in a sauce-pan over low heat. Cook until the mixture reaches a low rolling boil. Remove from heat.

Baste the chickens with the vinegar and spice mixture frequently after they have begun to brown. Baste and roast the chickens for an additional 30 minutes, or until the thickest portions can be pierced with a fork. Serves 8.

BARBECUED BROILERS #6

1 3-pound broiler, cut into portion-sized pieces
¼ cup peanut oil
½ cup chili sauce
½ cup lemon juice
½ teaspoon salt
½ teaspoon garlic powder
¼ teaspoon seasoned pepper (available in the spice section
   of most stores)
½ teaspoon celery seed
½ teaspoon dill seed

Brown the pieces of chicken in the oil. Place the chicken, skin side down, in a buttered baking dish with a tight-fitting cover.

Mix all the other ingredients in a saucepan. Cook over low heat for 8 minutes to blend flavors.

Pour the sauce over the pieces of chicken, cover and place in a 350° F. oven for 30 minutes. Then turn over each piece of chicken so that the skin side is up. Return to the 350° F. oven but do not cover. Bake for an additional 25 minutes, or until the thickest pieces of chicken can be pierced with a fork. Serves 4.

BARBECUED BROILERS #7

2 broiling chickens, approximately 2 pounds each, cut in half
   lengthwise
½ cup melted butter
2 tablespoons cider vinegar or wine vinegar
2 drops Tabasco
½ teaspoon salt
¼ teaspoon pepper
2 tablespoons Worcestershire sauce
½ teaspoon prepared mustard
¼ teaspoon sugar
½ teaspoon paprika

Preheat the oven at broil about 10 minutes before you start. Using a little of the melted butter, grease the rack of your broiling tray. Place the chicken, skin side down, on the rack.

To the remaining melted butter add the vinegar, Tabasco, salt, pepper, Worcestershire sauce, mustard, sugar and paprika. Mix all very well. Using a pastry brush, baste the exposed side of the chicken. Set the sauce aside for the second basting.

Place the chicken about 8 inches away from the broiler heat and broil for 15 minutes. Then turn the chicken pieces over and baste again. Broil for 20 minutes longer, basting from time to time until you have used up all of the sauce. Test for doneness by piercing the thickest part of the breast with a sharp fork. Serves 4. This chicken is excellent with parsley potatoes.

BARBECUED BROILERS #8

This recipe should be started the day before you intend serving it, for the chicken should marinate at least overnight.

4 2- to 3-pound broilers, cut in quarters
1 cup wine vinegar
1 cup Rhine wine
¼ pound butter
½ teaspoon seasoned pepper (found in the spice section of most stores)
¼ teaspoon thyme
¼ teaspoon rosemary
¼ teaspoon celery salt
¼ teaspoon garlic salt

Place the chicken pieces skin side down on the broiler pan rack. Place rack over broiler pan, then fill the pan with water to just below the rack. Cover tightly with aluminum foil. Be sure you have all the edges well sealed, for steam cooking is important. Place the chicken, thus sealed, in a 350° F. oven for 1¼ hours.

Mix the wine vinegar, wine, butter, seasoned pepper, thyme, rosemary, celery salt and garlic salt together in a saucepan. Place over low heat and cook until all the butter has melted.

Remove the steamed chicken from the oven. Discard the water in the broiler pan. Pour the vinegar and wine mixture in a large bowl with a tight-fitting cover. Place the chicken in the marinade while still hot. Let stand at least an hour. However, letting it stand in the marinade until it has become cool enough to put in the refrigerator is even better. Refrigerate overnight. Be sure each piece is coated with the marinade.

When you are ready to barbecue the chicken, turn the oven on to 350° F. Remove the chicken from the marinade and place in a shallow baking pan. Save the marinade for basting. Bake the chicken for 25 minutes longer, basting frequently with the marinade. The chicken should be golden brown and tender enough so you can pierce the thickest portions with a fork. Serves 8.

BROILERS IN ORANGE SAUCE

2 2- to 3-pound broilers, cut in half lengthwise
6 tablespoons butter
1 tablespoon prepared Dusseldorf-style mustard
1 4-ounce can frozen orange juice, thawed
½ cup brown sugar, tightly packed
2 tablespoons cornstarch
½ cup water
¼ cup vodka (optional)

Whip the butter and mustard together until very smooth and well blended. Rub this mixture over the inside and outside of the chicken. Place the chicken, skin side down, in a baking dish with a tight-fitting cover.

Mix together the orange juice and one can of water. Stir in the brown sugar and continue to stir until the sugar is all dissolved. Pour this over and around the chicken. Place in a 375° F. oven for 30 minutes. Then turn the chicken pieces over so they are skin side up; baste with the juice that has gathered in the bottom of the pan and continue to bake, uncovered, for 20 minutes longer. Baste from time to time.

Remove the chicken to a heated platter and place in a warmed oven while you make the sauce. Mix the cornstarch with the half cup of water. Stir this into the juices gathered in the bottom of the pan. Cook over low heat, stirring constantly, until thickened. Remove from the heat, stir in the vodka and pour over the chicken. Serve at once, piping hot. Serves 4.

Variation:

Use 1 cup of fresh squeezed orange juice if you do not have the frozen. Garnish with 1 4-ounce can of mandarin oranges, drained, for added flavor.

BROILERS WITH MUSHROOMS

2 1½ pound broilers, cut in half lengthwise
½ teaspoon salt
¼ teaspoon pepper
1 cup mushroom stems and pieces
1 10-ounce can cream of mushroom soup

Place the broiler halves skin side down in a suitable shallow buttered baking pan. Sprinkle them with salt and pepper. Distribute the mushroom stems and pieces around the chicken.

Using a pastry brush, coat each chicken generously with the cream of mushroom soup. Keep the remainder for coating the other side.

Place in a 350° F. oven for 20 minutes. Then turn over each piece of chicken and coat it with the remainder of the cream of mushroom soup. Continue cooking for another 20 minutes.

A few minutes before you are ready to serve, turn the oven to "broil" and brown the chicken to a rich golden brown. Serve piping hot. Serves 4.

BROILERS BAKED IN WINE

2 broilers, approximately 2 pounds each, cut in half lengthwise
2 cups dry white wine—sauterne or Chablis
¼ cup parsley, chopped fine
¼ cup onion, chopped fine
½ cup melted butter
½ teaspoon salt
¼ teaspoon pepper
1 teaspoon Accent
½ teaspoon paprika

The evening before you are going to serve this dish, place the chicken halves in a covered refrigerator dish with the wine, parsley and onion. Let the chicken marinate in the refrigerator overnight.

Next day, drain off the wine and set it aside. Preheat the oven to 400° F. Place the four halves of chicken, skin side down in a flat baking pan. In a saucepan, warm the wine in which you marinated the chicken. Add the melted butter, salt, pepper, Accent and paprika. Stir well so that all is mixed. Pour this mixture over the chicken halves. Place them in the preheated 400° F. oven for 20 minutes; baste the chicken frequently with the wine mixture.

Turn the chicken over so that the skin side is up; continue to bake for 20 minutes longer. Baste frequently during this period. Then test the thickest part of a breast to see if the chicken is tender and done. Place the chicken halves on a heated platter and pour the remaining wine sauce over them. Serves 4.

BAKED BROILERS WITH STUFFING

2 broilers, approximately 2 pounds each, cut in half lengthwise
1 teaspoon salt
½ teaspoon Accent
¼ teaspoon pepper
2½ cups fluffy cooked rice
¼ cup celery, chopped fine
¼ cup onion, chopped fine
¼ cup parsley, chopped fine
¼ teaspoon thyme
¼ teaspoon savory
¼ teaspoon marjoram
½ cup melted butter
1 10-ounce package mushrooms frozen in butter sauce
1 cup milk

Sprinkle the ribcage of each piece of chicken with some of the salt and the Accent. Rub the outside of the chicken with the remainder of the salt and the pepper.

Mix the rice, celery, onion, parsley, thyme, savory, marjoram and melted butter together. Divide into four equal portions and place a well-packed mound of the stuffing on the bottom of a buttered flat baking dish big enough to accommodate the chicken pieces. Place the ribcage of each broiler over the rice stuffing. Distribute the mushrooms around the pieces of chicken and then add the milk. Bake in a 350° F. oven for 30 minutes, basting from time to time with some of the juice that has gathered in the bottom of the pan. If the chicken is not sufficiently brown, turn on the broiler for a few seconds. Serve by using a wide spatula which you slide under each chicken piece in order to keep the rice filling intact from oven to plate. Serves 4.

BROILERS CHASSEURS

2 broilers, approximately 1½ pounds each, cut in half lengthwise
1 cup all-purpose flour
½ teaspoon pulverized thyme
½ teaspoon pulverized rosemary
½ teaspoon salt
¼ teaspoon pepper
6 to 8 tablespoons butter (for browning chicken)
1 cup mushroom stems and pieces
¼ cup onion, diced fine
Juice of ½ lemon
1 teaspoon brown sugar
1 medium-sized tart baking apple, peeled, quartered, cored
   and sliced into ⅛-inch pieces
2 medium-sized tomatoes, cut into ½-inch cubes
¼ cup chopped parsley
¼ cup chives, chopped fine

Place the flour, thyme, rosemary, salt and pepper in a
large paper sack. Shake to mix well. Place each half of the
chicken in the sack and shake it well so that the chicken is completely covered with the seasoned flour mixture.

Melt the butter in a large skillet with a tight-fitting cover.
Place the chicken, skin side down, in the skillet and brown
it evenly on both sides over moderate heat. Then add the
mushrooms and onion. Continue to cook for 5 minutes or
until the onion is glazed. Then add the lemon juice, brown
sugar, apple and tomatoes. Stir well so that all ingredients
are distributed around the chicken halves. Cover the pan
tightly and cook over low heat for 1 hour. Turn the chicken
pieces from time to time so that all of the flavors are well
blended. If the pan becomes too dry, add a tablespoon or two
of water.

At the end of this time the chicken should be tender enough
to pierce with a fork at the thickest part.

Place the chicken on a hot platter; arrange the mushrooms
and gravy around it; sprinkle the parsley and chives over
the top. Serve at once. Serves 4.

BAKED CHICKEN DINNER IN ONE PAN

2 broilers, approximately 2 pounds each, cut in half lengthwise
6 medium-sized potatoes, peeled and cut in quarters
3 tender young carrots, peeled and cut in ⅛-inch circles
3 small onions, peeled and cut in quarters
1 teaspoon salt
¼ teaspoon pepper
1 cup half and half cream
¼ pound butter

Place the vegetables in a roasting pan which has a tight-fitting cover and which will be large enough to accommodate all of the chicken too. Place the chicken halves over the vegetables.

Sprinkle with salt and pepper; pour all the cream over the chicken. Dot with squares of butter. Cover tightly and bake at 350° F. for 1 hour, or until you can pierce the thickest part of the chicken with a sharp fork. Uncover and place under the broiler for 5 minutes or until the chicken is a golden brown. Serve piping hot. Serves 4.

Chapter IV

ROAST CHICKEN

WE ALL HAVE a memory of a stuffed-to-bursting chicken with golden brown gravy. That bread dressing was a veritable dream. But nowadays it seems that stuffed roast chicken is not as popular as it once was. If you have not made one for your family for a long time, you should give it a whirl.

This is a most economical, easy way to serve chicken, and it is a great budget stretcher to boot. Chicken does not always have to be stuffed with bread dressing as you will find in glancing through this chapter. There are many other wonderful foods which, when used for stuffing, make good companions to roasted chicken.

Today's roasting chickens are younger and more tender than those labeled "stewing chickens." Their weight is usually between 4 and 6 pounds. If you can find a roasting capon you have a taste thrill coming.

Never, never stuff a chicken the day before you roast it. You run great danger of food poisoning if you try stuffing a bird too far in advance of roasting. If you know you are going to be in a bind for time, you can make the stuffing and store it separately in your refrigerator until you are ready to roast the bird. This is true for all stuffed fowl.

When stuffing a chicken, always use a light touch. Spoon the filling in lightly; never pack it tight. While roasting, the filling expands, and this may make the chicken split its sides. If you have overshot your mark and made too much filling, you can bake it separately in a baking dish. It will be delicious with the gravy.

Should you have any leftovers after the chicken has been served, always remove the stuffing from the cavity. It is wise too to remove all the meat from the bones before you refrigerate it.

The danger of food poisoning is always present; do not take a chance. After you have stripped the bird of stuffing and meat you can make an excellent broth from the bones. (See Chapter #5, "Chicken Soups.")

Once you start roasting a chicken, follow through until it is done. Never remove a half-roasted, stuffed bird from the oven with the idea that you will complete the roasting the next day. You are just courting trouble. Harmful, poisonous bacteria would find this an excellent place to grow and thrive.

CHICKEN STUFFED WITH RICE

1 4-pound roasting chicken
¼ cup soy sauce
½ teaspoon Accent
¼ cup melted butter
1 cup instant precooked packaged rice
2 cups celery, cut diagonally in ⅛-inch pieces
½ cup chopped onion
1 8-ounce can mushroom stems and pieces, do not drain
½ cup chopped parsley
¼ pound butter, softened to room temperature
½ cup honey

Preheat oven to 475° F. Brush the inside of the chicken with the soy sauce. Sprinkle the cavity with Accent and then set the chicken aside.

Melt the butter in a large skillet; add the rice just as it comes from the package and sauté until the rice is golden brown. Add the celery, onion, mushrooms and parsley. Cook over low heat until the celery becomes soft and glazed. Remove from heat and allow to cool.

Stuff the cavity of the chicken with the celery and rice mixture. Truss the opening tightly with skewers or by sewing with string. Place the chicken in a roasting pan that has a tight-fitting cover. Beat the butter and honey together with a slotted spoon. Coat the entire chicken with this mixture and place it *uncovered* in the 475° F. oven. Bake at 475° F. for 25 minutes, basting occasionally with the browned honey and butter which gathers in the bottom of the pan. Turn oven down to 350° F. Place chicken breast side down and cover and bake for 1 hour. Then turn chicken over so that the legs are pointing up. Baste once more with the browned butter and honey in the bottom of the pan. Cover again and bake for 1 hour longer, or until a fork can pierce the thickest part of the breast. Serve piping hot. Serves 4.

Note: The moisture from the celery and onions puffs up the rice inside of the chicken.

ROAST CHICKEN IN FOIL

2 broiler chickens, approximately 2 pounds in weight, cut in
  half lengthwise
2 sticks of butter or margarine
2 envelopes dry onion soup mix
Enough aluminum foil to wrap tightly
4 cups hot fluffy cooked rice

Place the chicken halves on aluminum foil large enough to
bring up over the top and wrap tightly; or use two pieces of
foil, one for the bottom and one for the top.

Cut the butter into ¼-inch slices and arrange them over
the top of the chicken. Sprinkle with the dry onion soup mix.
Cover tightly with aluminum foil, making sure that no steam
will be able to escape during cooking.

Place in a 300° F. oven for 45 minutes. Open one corner
of the foil and test for doneness by piercing the thickest part
of the chicken with a fork. Serve with a portion of the rice.
Use a spoonful of the gathered juices in the bottom of the
foil to top the rice. Serves 4.

ROAST CHICKEN IN BRANDY SAUCE

1 4- to 6-pound roasting chicken
½ teaspoon salt
¼ teaspoon pepper
6 tablespoons butter
¼ cup onion, chopped fine
¾ cup brandy
½ cup heavy cream
1 tablespoon minced parsley

Cut the chicken into serving pieces. Sprinkle with salt and
pepper. Melt the butter in an ovenproof skillet and brown
the pieces of chicken in it evenly over moderate heat.

Add the onion and continue to cook until it is tender and
glazed. Add the brandy and turn each piece of chicken so
that it is coated with brandy.

Cover the pan tightly with aluminum foil and place in a
350° F. oven for 25 minutes. Then remove the foil and pour
the cream into the chicken mixture. Continue to cook at
350° F. for 5 minutes longer. Serve at once, piping hot, garnished with the minced parsley. Serves 4 to 6.

ROAST CHICKEN WITH WATER
CHESTNUT STUFFING

1 3½ to 5-pound roasting chicken or capon
1 teaspoon salt
1 teaspoon Accent
¼ teaspoon pepper
12 slices stale white bread
1 cup milk
½ pound lean ground pork
½ pound chicken livers
¾ cup apple, coarsely chopped
¼ cup onion, chopped fine
1 #½ can water chestnuts, drained and cut into ⅛-inch slices
¼ teaspoon seasoned pepper (available in the spice section
   of most stores)
2 eggs, beaten until lemon yellow

Wipe the chicken, inside and out, with paper toweling. Mix the salt, Accent and pepper together and rub the chicken inside and out with the mixture. Set chicken aside while you make the stuffing.

Break up the slices of bread and soak in the milk. Turn the mixture over from time to time so that all the bread gets a chance to absorb some of the milk.

Place the ground pork in a skillet and sauté until a light brown. Remove the pork from the skillet and place the chicken livers in the fat that is left. Sauté the chicken livers until they are tender and just beginning to brown, then remove from the heat and allow them to cool. When cool, chop them coarsely and mix with the sautéed ground pork. Save the remaining fat for brushing the outside of the chicken.

Squeeze out any excess milk from the bread; discard the leftover milk. Add the chicken livers and pork to the bread along with the apple and onion. Mix well. Add the water chestnuts and seasoned pepper. Add the eggs and stir all with a light hand. Stuff the cavity of the chicken with this mixture. Close opening with skewers or sew with string. Tie the chicken legs together. Brush the outside of the chicken with the fat that is left in the skillet after frying the chicken livers. If there is not sufficient fat, use a little melted butter or margarine.

Place chicken, breast side down, in a roasting pan with a tight-fitting cover; roast at 350° F. for 1 hour. Then turn chicken over, breast side up, and continue to roast for an additional hour. Remove cover and bake for an additional

25 minutes to allow browning. Test for doneness by piercing the thickest portions of the chicken with a sharp fork. Serve at once, piping hot. If you like gravy with your chicken, add 1 cup water and 1 tablespoon instant chicken bouillon to the drippings in the roasting pan; add 2 tablespoons cornstarch dissolved in another ½ cup water. Cook over low heat until thickened. Serves 4.

Variations:

Add 1 cup of toasted almonds, coarsely chopped, to the dressing.
Add 1 cup of toasted pecans, coarsely chopped, to the dressing.
Substitute ½ pound of mixed chicken giblets for chicken livers.
Substitute ½ pound of ground chuck for the pork; sauté in 3 tablespoons of butter until a rich brown

BAKED CHICKEN WITH A ZIP

Most people look at you in horror when you tell them to bake chicken in vinegar; what they fail to remember is that cooking reduces the sourness of any vinegar-flavored dish. This way of making chicken is a delight, for you have the heartiness of good chicken flavor plus a certain tartness that only vinegar can impart.

1 3-pound fryer-broiler, cut into portion-sized pieces
1 teaspoon salt
1 teaspoon pepper
½ teaspoon Accent
¾ cup cider vinegar
3 Winesap apples, cored and cut into quarters

Dry the pieces of chicken with paper toweling; sprinkle with the salt, pepper and Accent. Place in a lightly buttered baking dish, skin side down. Pour in the vinegar, and arrange the apple pieces, skin side up, around the chicken. Place in a 325° F. oven for 1 hour. Then lift up the foil and turn the pieces of chicken over, skin side up. Turn the apples over so that they are resting on their skins. Cover with the foil again and continue to bake at 325° F. for an additional 1 hour and 15 minutes, or until the thickest portions can be easily pierced with a fork. Serve at once, piping hot. Serves 4.

ROAST CHICKEN WITH SAVORY RICE STUFFING

1 3- to 5-pound roasting chicken or capon
1 teaspoon salt
1 teaspoon Accent
¼ teaspoon pepper
3 tablespoons butter
½ cup onion, chopped fine
½ cup celery, chopped fine
2 cups boiling water with 2 tablespoons instant chicken bouillon dissolved in it
½ teaspoon pulverized sage
2 tablespoons dehydrated parsley flakes
1 cup instant rice as it comes from the package
1 4-ounce can mushroom stems and pieces, drained

Wipe the chicken inside and out with paper toweling. Mix the salt, Accent and pepper together. Rub the chicken inside and out with the mixture.

Melt the butter in a skillet with a tight-fitting cover. Add the onion and sauté until it is transparent and glazed. Add the celery and the boiling water. Add the sage, parsley flakes and rice. Bring to a rolling boil and then turn heat back to simmer. Cover and cook for 15 minutes without stirring. Remove from the heat, stir in the mushrooms and allow to cool for a few minutes.

Place the rice mixture in the cavity of the chicken. Fasten the openings with skewers or by sewing. Place the chicken, breast side down, in a roasting pan with a tight-fitting cover. Cover and bake for 1 hour at 350° F. Then turn chicken breast side up, and continue to bake, covered, at 350° F. for an additional hour. Remove cover to allow chicken to brown and bake for an additional 25 minutes at 350° F., or until the thickest portion of the chicken can be easily pierced with a fork. Serves 4.

Variations:

For gravy, add 1 cup water to the pan drippings along with 1 tablespoon instant chicken bouillon. Bring to a boil and loosen the browned juices from the bottom of the pan. Thicken by stirring in ½ cup water in which 1 tablespoon cornstarch has been dissolved.

Another delicious gravy can be made by adding ½ cup water to the pan drippings; bring to a rolling boil to loosen the browned juices. Then add 1 can (10-ounce) cream of chicken soup. Stir and blend and heat through.

ROAST CHICKEN SUPREME

1 3-pound fryer-broiler, cut into portion-sized pieces
½ cup all-purpose flour
½ teaspoon salt
¼ teaspoon pepper
1 teaspoon paprika
½ cup vegetable oil
2 cups instant rice
1 10-ounce can cream of celery soup
1 10-ounce can cream of mushroom soup
1 cup milk
1 envelope onion soup mix

Wipe the pieces of chicken with paper toweling. Mix the flour, salt, pepper and paprika together and sprinkle over the pieces of chicken until they are lightly covered. Heat the oil in a large skillet and brown each piece of chicken on all sides. Remove from heat and set aside.

Sprinkle the instant rice, just as it comes from the package, over the bottom of a well-buttered 9″ x 13″ baking pan. Put the celery soup, mushroom soup and milk in a saucepan; stir well and heat to just below boiling point. Pour this soup mixture over the instant rice. Place the pieces of browned chicken on top of the rice and soup and then sprinkle it with the onion soup mix. Discard any pan drippings left from browning the chicken.

Cover the baking pan with aluminum foil, making sure that the seal is perfect so no steam can escape. Place in a 300° F. oven for 2 hours, or until the thickest piece of chicken can be pierced with a fork. Serve at once, piping hot. Serves 4.

Variations:

Use 1 10-ounce can of cream of chicken soup for either the mushroom or celery soup.
Use two 10-ounce cans of cream of chicken soup for the mushroom and celery soups.

OLD-FASHIONED STUFFED ROAST CHICKEN

1 4- to 6-pound roasting chicken or capon
1 teaspoon Accent
½ cup butter
½ cup onion, chopped fine
¼ cup parsley, chopped fine
6 cups day-old bread, cubed in ½-inch pieces
½ teaspoon pulverized sage
¼ teaspoon marjoram
¼ teaspoon thyme
1½ teaspoons celery seed
½ teaspoon salt
¼ teaspoon pepper
¼ cup additional melted butter (for outside of the chicken)
3 tablespoons flour
½ teaspoon paprika

Sprinkle the cavity of the chicken with Accent and set aside. Place the giblets in 1 cup of water in a saucepan and cook on top of the stove until they are tender. Chop them coarsely. Reserve the liquid until later.

Melt the butter in a large skillet; add the onion and cook until it becomes glazed. Add the parsley, bread cubes, giblets, sage, marjoram, thyme, celery seed, salt and pepper and cook over low heat, mixing well while cooking. The bread cubes should be warmed through. Add ½ cup of the giblet broth, then mix until it is well distributed.

Spoon the filling into the neck cavity and into the large cavity with a light touch. Using skewers and string, close both openings securely. Place the chicken in a roasting pan. Mix the melted butter, flour and paprika and brush this over the outside skin of the chicken.

Place the chicken in a 350° F. oven for approximately 3 hours. When it is done, the thickest portion of the breast should pierce easily with a fork.

Remove the chicken from the roasting pan to a hot platter. Return to the warm oven while you make the gravy, as follows:

Place the roasting pan over low heat and add the remainder of the giblet water. This should be about ½ cup. Add an additional ¾ cup of water. Using a slotted spoon, cook and stir until you have loosened all the browned juice from the bottom of the pan. There should be sufficient thickening left from the flour that you spread on the outside of the chicken with the butter and paprika. If not, mix 2 tablespoons of flour with the water before you add it to the pan drippings. Cook until thickened, stirring all the while. Serve piping hot with the chicken. Serves 4 to 6.

PARMESAN-ROMANO CHICKEN BAKE

2 2- to 3-pound fryer-broiler, cut into portion-sized pieces
2 eggs, beaten until lemon yellow
2 cups bread crumbs, rolled fine
½ cup Romano cheese, grated fine
½ cup Parmesan cheese, grated fine
½ cup green pepper, chopped fine
½ cup celery, chopped fine
½ teaspoon salt
½ teaspoon orégano
¼ pound butter

Dry the chicken pieces on paper toweling. Dip each piece into the beaten eggs.

Mix the bread crumbs, cheeses, green pepper, celery, salt and orégano in a paper sack. Put each piece of egg-dipped chicken into this crumb mixture and shake vigorously until thoroughly coated. Press coating onto the chicken so it will adhere.

Melt two tablespoons of the butter and spread over the bottom of a large flat baking pan. Place the chicken in the melted butter, skin side down. Dot with chips of butter, then cover the pan tightly with aluminum foil. Bake for 45 minutes at 350° F.

Then remove the aluminum foil, turn the pieces of chicken over and continue to bake for an additional 30 minutes at 350° F., or until a rich golden brown and tender enough to pierce with a fork at the thickest portions. Serves 6.

Variations:

Use all Romano cheese instead of a mixture of Romano and Parmesan.
Use all Parmesan cheese instead of a mixture of Romano and Parmesan.

ROAST CHICKEN WITH POMEGRANATE STUFFING

1 3- to 4-pound roasting chicken
1 cup (tightly packed) lean ground chuck or round steak
1 cup coarsely chopped sweet onions
½ cup boiling water with 2 tablespoons instant chicken bouillon dissolved in it
½ teaspoon salt
¼ teaspoon pepper
¼ teaspoon allspice
¼ teaspoon cinnamon
¼ teaspoon freshly grated nutmeg
1 cup pomegranate juice, unsweetened (Available in the gourmet section of your supermarket or in health food stores. Two fresh pomegranates will yield about 1 cup of juice if put through a cone-shaped food press.)
1 tablespoon light brown sugar
2 tablespoons lemon juice
1 tablespoon cider vinegar
1 lemon, cut in half

Remove the fat from the inside of the chicken and cut it up into small pieces. Place the fat in a large skillet and render it over low heat. If you are unfortunate enough to get a chicken without any spare fat, use 4 tablespoons peanut oil. Remove the crisp pieces of tissue from the fat and discard after rendering. Place the ground beef in the chicken fat and sauté until golden brown. Push the beef to one side and sauté the onions until they are transparent and just beginning to brown. Pour off any excess fat. Add the water and bouillon and bring to a rolling boil, stirring frequently to remove all the browned meat from the bottom of the skillet. Continue to cook until the water has disappeared.

Add the salt, pepper, allspice, cinnamon, nutmeg and pomegranate juice. Stir in the sugar, lemon juice and vinegar and then remove from the heat.

Using half of the lemon for the inside, rub the chicken until its juice is all used up. Using the other half of lemon, rub the outside of the chicken until its juice is used up.

Stuff the meat, vegetable and pomegranate juice mixture inside the chicken and seal shut with skewers. Place the chicken, breast side down, in a roasting pan with a tight-fitting cover. Bake at 325° F. for 1 hour. Then turn the chicken over, breast side up, and bake for an additional hour. Baste from time to time with the juice that has gathered in the bottom of the pan. Remove the cover at the end of this second hour, and bake for another 35 minutes uncovered in order to permit the chicken to turn golden brown. Again baste with pan juices from time to time.

Serve piping hot. Serves 6.

Garnish with seedless green grapes on each end of the platter for an unusual flavor combination.

ORANGE-STUFFED CHICKEN

1 4- to 5-pound roasting chicken
½ teaspoon Accent
¼ teaspoon pepper
½ teaspoon salt
3 seedless oranges, peeled and sliced into ½-inch slices
¾ cup celery, cut diagonally into ½-inch pieces
¼ cup chopped parsley
½ cup dry white wine
½ cup orange juice
¼ cup honey
4 cups hot cooked fluffy rice
2 tablespoons cornstarch mixed in ½ cup water

Dry the chicken inside and out with paper toweling. Sprinkle the cavity with Accent; rub the outside with pepper and salt. Mix the sliced oranges, celery and parsley together and place in the cavity of the chicken. Truss with skewers; tie legs together so that chicken can be placed breast side down in the roasting pan.

Place chicken in the roasting pan. Mix the white wine and orange juice and pour this around the chicken. Brush the chicken with honey. Place in a 425° F. oven, uncovered, for 40 minutes. Baste occasionally. At the end of this time, turn the chicken over, breast side up, and roast at 350° F. for an additional 30 minutes. Baste the breast and legs frequently during this time.

To serve, place the chicken in the middle of a heated platter with the rice mounded around the outside. Skim off any excess fat from the liquid in the pan and then stir in the cornstarch and water. Cook over low heat, stirring constantly, until quite thick. Pour this thickened gravy over the mounded rice. Serves 6.

ROAST CHICKEN WITH TOASTED ALMOND STUFFING

1 3- to 5-pound roasting chicken or capon
1 teaspoon salt
1 teaspoon Accent
¼ teaspoon pepper
12 slices day-old enriched white bread
1 cup boiling water with 2 tablespoons instant chicken bouillon
   dissolved in it
4 tablespoons butter
1 cup slivered almonds
¼ cup onion, chopped fine
¼ cup parsley, chopped fine
¼ cup celery, chopped fine
⅛ teaspoon pulverized sage
1 egg, slightly beaten

Wipe the chicken, inside and out with paper toweling. Mix the salt, Accent and pepper together. Rub the outside and inside of the chicken with this mixture. Set aside while you prepare the stuffing.

Break up the pieces of bread and pour the cup of boiling water and chicken bouillon over them. Turn the mixture from time to time so that all the bread becomes saturated.

Melt the butter in a large skillet. Add the almonds and sauté until they become golden brown. Push the almonds off to one side of the skillet and add the onion. Sauté the onion until it is glazed and transparent. Add the parsley, celery and sage. Mix all very well, then remove from heat.

Squeeze the bread mixture until fairly dry; discard any of the bouillon water that is left. Add the almonds and vegetables to the bread mixture. Mix well, and then stir in the slightly beaten egg. Mix with a light hand. Stuff the cavity of the chicken with the mixture. Close the opening with skewers or by sewing. Put the chicken, breast side down, in a roaster with a tight-fitting cover. Place in a 350° F. oven for 1 hour. Then turn the chicken over, breast side up, and continue to roast at 350° F. for an additional hour. Remove the cover and bake, uncovered, for an additional 25 minutes, or until the chicken is a delicate golden brown and the thickest portion can be easily pierced with a sharp fork. Serves 4.

Variations:

Should you want a delicately flavored gravy for this chicken, add ½ cup water to the pan drippings, plus 10-ounce can cream of chicken soup. Heat and blend until smooth.

Substitute 1 cup of coarsely chopped hazel nuts for the almonds.

Substitute 1 cup of coarsely chopped pecans for the almonds.

Substitute 1 cup of coarsely chopped Brazil nuts for the almonds, then drain off any excess butter left in the pan after toasting, for Brazil nuts have enough natural oil.

ROAST CHICKEN WITH WINE

1 4-pound roasting chicken, cut in half lengthwise
¼ cup melted butter
1 cup small button mushrooms
1 cup cubed lean ham
1 cup small white onions
1 teaspoon salt
¼ teaspoon pepper
1 cup dry white wine

Put the chicken in a roasting pan, skin side up. Brush with melted butter and place under the broiler until it is golden brown. Then turn the oven down to 350° F.

Arrange the mushrooms, ham and onions around the chicken. Sprinkle with salt and pepper. Add the white wine. Cover the pan tightly with aluminum foil and return it to the 350° F. oven. Bake for 1 hour.

If you like the flavor of chicken liver, cut it up raw and add it to the mushrooms, etc., around the chicken during the roasting time.

During the last 5 minutes of cooking, remove the aluminum foil to recrisp the outside of the chicken. Serve piping hot. Serves 4.

ROAST CHICKEN WITH VEGETABLE STUFFING

1 3- to 5-pound roasting chicken or capon
1 teaspoon Accent
1 teaspoon salt
¼ teaspoon pepper
1 10-ounce package frozen chopped spinach, thawed and
   drained
¾ cup grated raw carrot
½ cup onion, diced fine
¼ cup green pepper, chopped fine
½ cup celery, chopped fine
¼ cup parsley, chopped fine
2 cups soft whole wheat bread crumbs
2 tablespoons rendered chicken fat or butter
2 eggs, slightly beaten
3 tablespoons melted butter

Dry the chicken, inside and out, with paper toweling. Mix
the Accent, salt and pepper and rub this mixture over the
inside and outside of the chicken. Set chicken aside while
you make the stuffing.

Mix together the spinach, carrot, onion, green pepper,
celery and parsley. Add the bread crumbs and the chicken
fat and mix again. Stir in the beaten eggs with a light touch.

Stuff the chicken with the vegetable dressing; close the
opening with skewers or sew with string. Tie legs together.

Brush the outside of the chicken with the melted butter
and place, breast side down, in a roasting pan with a cover.
Bake, covered, at 350° F. for 1 hour. Then turn the chicken
over, breast side up, and continue to bake at 350° F. for an
additional hour. Remove cover and bake for 25 minutes longer
at 350° F. so that the breast can become a delicate brown.
Test for doneness by piercing the thickest parts with a sharp
fork. Serves 4.

ROAST CHICKEN WITH RAISIN STUFFING

1 4- to 6-pound roasting chicken or capon
1 teaspoon Accent
4 tablespoons butter
¾ cup onion, chopped fine
½ teaspoon pulverized sage
1 cup seedless raisins
¼ cup water
5 cups ½" x ½" bread cubes (no crusts included)
½ teaspoon salt
¼ teaspoon pepper
1 egg, beaten until lemon yellow
¼ cup melted butter (for outside of chicken)
2 tablespoons flour

Sprinkle the cavity of the chicken with the Accent and then set aside while you are preparing the filling.

Melt the butter in a large skillet; add the onion and sauté until it is glazed and transparent. Add the sage, raisins and water; simmer for 5 minutes. Pour this mixture over the bread cubes and mix very well.

Add the salt, pepper and egg. Mix again to distribute the egg and seasonings evenly. Spoon the stuffing into the chicken with a light hand. Close and truss the opening with skewers and string.

Mix the melted butter and the flour; lavishly brush the outside of the chicken with the mixture. Roast in a 350° F. oven for 3 hours, or until a fork will easily pierce the thickest part of the breast. Serve piping hot. Serves 6.

If you want gravy with this chicken, add ½ cup of water to the browned juice in the bottom of the roasting pan. Simmer until all the brown material is loosened. Then add an additional ½ cup of water into which you have stirred 1 tablespoon cornstarch. Cook until thick.

PEACHY-KEEN CHICKEN ROAST

2 3-pound broilers, cut into portion-sized pieces
1 #2½ can peach halves in heavy syrup (drain, but reserve syrup)
2 tablespoons onion, chopped fine
2 tablespoons soy sauce
½ cup butter or margarine
1 teaspoon Accent
12 maraschino cherries

In a large flat roasting pan place the pieces of chicken, skin side up, without letting them overlap.

In a saucepan, heat the syrup from the peaches to just below boiling point. Add the chopped onion, soy sauce, butter or margarine and Accent. Baste each piece of chicken generously with this mixture. Place in a 375° F. oven for 1½ hours, basting frequently. When the chicken is golden brown and tender enough to pierce with a fork, place the peach halves, hole side up, around the chicken. Place a cherry in the center of each peach. Return to the oven for an additional 8 minutes or until the peaches are warmed through. Serves 8.

ROAST CHICKEN IN RHINE WINE AND VODKA

1 3-pound fryer-broiler, cut into portion-sized pieces
1 teaspoon salt
¼ teaspoon pepper
¾ cup Rhine wine
½ cup vodka

Place the chicken, skin side down, in a lightly buttered baking pan. Sprinkle the pieces with salt and pepper. Pour in the Rhine wine and vodka. Cover the pan tightly with aluminum foil.

Place in a 325° F. oven for 1 hour and 15 minutes; then lift up the foil, turn the pieces of chicken over, skin side up, and bake at 325° F. for 1 more hour, or until the thickest pieces of chicken can be pierced with a fork. Remove the foil during the last 10 minutes of baking to brown the chicken and reduce the liquids. Serve at once, piping hot. Serves 4.

Chapter V
CHICKEN SOUPS

CHICKEN SOUP IS the only soup that can be called an international favorite. Originally this was a matter of pure economy.

If a chicken happily traipsed around the barnyard clucking and laying eggs every day as she's supposed to, nobody bothered her. But let that happy hen take an egg vacation, and she ended up in the soup kettle in nothing flat. Being called a "soup chicken" is probably the nastiest phrase in hen talk.

These nonlaying hens under compulsory retirement did and still do make good soup. However, modern chicken-raising and marketing methods have added an euphemism to the name. Today they are usually referred to as "stewing chickens."

Since every well-organized barnyard should have only one rooster to crow at dawn, we will not go into whether they end up as "stewing chickens" or not. The only thing that can be said for roosters is that there are farms where all the poor bird's sex privileges are removed and he ends up being called a capon. Capons are full-breasted and make wonderful soup too. However, their real calling is in the realm of roast chicken or, if young, fried chicken.

If you make your chicken soup from a stewing chicken, it is going to need several hours of cooking time, since the bird is not young and tender to begin with. However, good chicken soup can also be made from less mature birds. The cooking time, naturally, is shorter, and the tender meat from the younger chicken is often part of the soup.

If your family likes chicken soup, do not pass up the wonderful bargains found in today's market in backs, necks and wings. You can buy pounds of these for a fraction of what a whole chicken costs, and the flavor of necks, backs and wings is great and hearty.

Usually these pieces are taken from fryer-broilers that are sold in packages of separate breasts or legs and thighs. Here again is an additional saving, for these parts do not need the long cooking time that the older stewing chicken does. Too, they do not have the surplus portions of rich yellow fat that most older stewing chickens possess.

If you do accumulate any amount of chicken fat from a

47

stewing chicken, do not despair. It freezes beautifully, whether it is rendered or raw, and can be put to almost the same use as butter in your cooking. Chicken fat is wonderful for frying potatoes or for frying other pieces of fryer chicken.

If you boast a home freezer, and come across a real bargain in backs, necks and wings, go all out and cook ten or fifteen pounds into a delicious chicken broth. Cool it, then pour it into disposable milk cartons and freeze it. When you need chicken broth, all you have to do is cut off both ends of the carton and slide this king-sized ice cube of chicken broth into your waiting kettle.

If you have a stockpile of this inexpensive chicken broth, making chicken soup will be a matter of minutes from freezer to stove. This soup stock can be augmented with noodles, dumplings or egg drops, and you can march to the table with palate-pleasing soup that your guests will think you worked on half the afternoon.

The very first recipe in this chapter will be for making a good chicken broth from necks, backs and wings. It is a very basic recipe. Should you want to multiply it, all you have to do is double, triple or quadruple the amounts of the ingredients given.

There are many versions of the universal favorite, chicken soup, which could not be included because, frankly, a whole book could be written about this soup alone. We have given you some important variations in the hope that you'll become an experimenter in the world of chicken soup-making and will try new ingredients and variations of your own.

The second recipe in this chapter is one with an eye to economy. It deals with making soup from the bones of a roast chicken. Most good cooks hate to see perfectly good roast chicken bones get thrown away. After all, they still have a lot of good nourishment left in them which the roasting did not even touch; and they do make a deliciously tasty soup.

CHICKEN BROTH—A BASIC RECIPE

5 pounds chicken necks, backs and wings
½ cup coarsely chopped onion
2 carrots, peeled but left whole
5 stalks celery, cut into 2-inch lengths
1 tablespoon chopped parsley
1 teaspoon salt
½ teaspoon pepper
Cold water to cover

1 1-pound veal knuckle (optional—add this if you want a thick soup that will jell when cold)

Place all the ingredients in a large soup kettle with a tight-fitting cover. Bring to a rolling boil and skim off any froth that may gather on top. Turn the heat back to simmer, cover and cook for 2 hours.

Strain the broth and cool to room temperature, then place in the refrigerator to chill. Skim off any fat that has solidified on the surface of the soup after refrigerating, and save for frying.

This basic soup broth can be made into chicken rice, chicken noodle or chicken dumpling soup just by heating and adding the garnish you wish. It freezes wonderfully for future use. Just pour the chilled soup into disposable quart milk cartons and freeze. When you want to use the soup, just cut off both ends of the carton, push out the block of soup and heat.

This recipe makes approximately 2½ quarts of basic broth —6 average servings. For delicious garnishes for this broth, see Golden Chicken Soup—Jewish Style elsewhere in this chapter.

CHICKEN-CORN CHOWDER

4 pounds chicken wings
8 cups cold water
1 teaspoon salt
2 10-ounce packages frozen corn niblets
¼ teaspoon black pepper
¼ cup parsley, chopped fine

Place the chicken wings, water and salt in a soup kettle. Bring to a rolling boil, and remove any froth which may gather on top. Reduce heat to simmer and cook, covered, for 1½ hours.

Strain soup and allow the chicken wings to cool. Remove the meat from the bones. Discard the bones and the skin. Return the meat to the broth and again place over the heat. Bring to a simmer again and add the corn and black pepper. Cook for 15 minutes longer. Stir in the chopped parsley just before serving. Do not cover after the addition of the parsley or you will spoil its bright green color. Serve piping hot with oyster crackers. Serves 6.

CREAM OF CHICKEN SOUP SUPREME

1 3- to 5-pound stewing chicken, cut up
1 2-pound veal knuckle (have butcher crack it into 4 or 5 pieces)
2 tablespoons butter
2 carrots, scrubbed and scraped, cut into ¼-inch pieces
¼ cup chopped parsley
¾ cup diced celery
¼ teaspoon black pepper
1 small onion, diced
10 cups cold water
1 cup heavy cream
3 tablespoons instant flour
3 egg yolks, beaten until lemon yellow
½ teaspoon salt
2 drops Tabasco (optional)

Place the chicken, veal knuckle and butter in a large soup kettle. Lightly brown the outside of the chicken in the butter and the fat that will gather from the chicken and veal knuckle. Then add the carrots, parsley, celery, pepper, onion and cold water. Continue to cook until it starts to boil. Remove any surplus fat and froth that may gather on the top. Turn the heat down and continue to simmer for 2 to 3 hours, or until a fork can be twisted in the meat of the chicken breast.

Remove the chicken and veal bones from the soup. Set them aside to cool. Strain the soup through a fine sieve and set it aside to cool. As soon as it is cooled, carefully remove all of the fat from the surface. Then return the soup to the stove and bring to a simmer again.

Remove all the meat from the chicken bones. Discard all the skin and vegetable pieces, for you have already extracted all of the good in them.

Beat the cream, flour and eggs together until all are smoothly blended. Add the salt to the simmering soup and mix well. Take about ½ cup of the hot simmering soup and beat it into the egg and cream mixture. Then slowly add the egg-cream mixture to the soup, stirring all the while. Continue to cook over low heat for a few minutes longer, until the soup has thickened and lightly coats the spoon. At this point add the Tabasco if you like this sharpness in creamed soups. Serve piping hot with saltines. Serves 6 generously.

CHICKEN BONE SOUP FROM ROAST CHICKEN BONES

Usually I am very much opposed to making a poor chicken do double duty—especially after everyone has smacked his lips over some delightful main dish. However, there is one exception to this. If you have roasted a large chicken or capon, and all you have left is the bones, there is no reason why you shouldn't make a delicious soup from them. Here is the recipe:

All the bones left from a roasted chicken or capon (be sure
   the ribcage is scraped clear of all filling; rinse if necessary)
1 medium-sized carrot, peeled and cut into circles
½ cup sliced onion
½ cup coarsely chopped celery
2 tablespoons chopped parsley
1 teaspoon salt
¼ teaspoon pepper
8 cups cold water

Place the bones, carrot, onion, celery, parsley, salt, pepper and cold water in a soup kettle with a tight-fitting cover. Bring to a rolling boil, skimming off any froth that may gather. Turn the heat back to simmer, cover and continue to cook at low heat for 2½ hours. Strain and discard the vegetables. Any little particles of meat that may cling to the bones can be added to the broth. Serve as a simple clear broth or add noodles, dumplings or rice. See the garnishes for Golden Chicken Soup—Jewish Style for noodle and dumpling recipes. Makes 2 quarts of soup, enough for 4 generous servings.

EGG DROPS FOR CHICKEN SOUP

2 eggs, beaten until lemon yellow
6 level tablespoons all-purpose flour
½ cup cold water
¼ teaspoon salt

After the eggs have been beaten, continue to beat while adding the flour and cold water alternately. Add the salt and beat until all is well mixed. Drop this mixture from the end of a teaspoon into the rapidly boiling chicken broth. Continue to boil until the egg drops rise to the top, fluffy and golden. Serve at once.

ITALIAN STYLE CHICKEN SOUP

2 pounds chicken backs, necks and wings
1 pound soupbone, either beef or veal
1 pound lean stewing beef
2 stalks celery, cut into 2-inch pieces
2 medium-sized carrots, left whole
¼ cup coarsely chopped parsley
1 leek, about 1½-inch diameter, cut in ½-inch slices up to
    green part
¼ cup tomato sauce (optional)
1 teaspoon salt
½ teaspoon pepper
12 cups cold water

Put all of the ingredients in a large soup kettle and bring
to a rolling boil. Using a slotted spoon, skim of the froth that
gathers on top. Turn the heat back to simmer, cover, and
cook for 3 hours

Strain the soup and pick out only the lean morsels of meat;
discard the rest, for you have extracted all the good from them.
Let the broth cool to room temperature, then put it in the
coolest part of your refrigerator for several hours. Remove
the hardened fat that gathers at the top during this chilling;
discard it.

This soup may be served as a clear broth before a meal,
or as a hearty soup by adding the morsels of meat, noodles
or Italian Egg Fluff, recipe for which follows.

This is a rich soup mixture, so it may be watered down
with the addition of more water. Of course this depends on
your own taste and the type of meal you are going to serve
it with. Serves 6.

ITALIAN EGG FLUFF FOR ITALIAN
STYLE CHICKEN SOUP

4 eggs, separated
6 tablespoons grated Parmesan cheese
⅛ teaspoon freshly grated nutmeg
⅛ teaspoon salt

Beat the egg whites until they stand in peaks. Beat the egg
yolks until they are lemon yellow. Add the cheese, nutmeg
and salt to the beaten yolks and mix well. Fold the egg yolk
mixture into the beaten egg whites.

Have the soup boiling rapidly; drop the egg-cheese mixture into it by spoonful. The moment you have put in the last of the egg mixture, cover the soup and remove from the heat. Let stand for 5 minutes and then serve. Serves 6.

ITALIAN EGG AND CHICKEN BROTH

2 pounds chicken backs, necks and wings
1 veal knuckle, approximately 1 pound in weight, cracked
2 carrots, peeled but left whole
½ cup coarsely chopped celery
1 tablespoon chopped parsley
1 leek, about 1½-inch diameter, cut in ½-inch slices up to the
   green
½ teaspoon salt
¼ teaspoon pepper
5 cups cold water
4 slices enriched white bread, lightly buttered
4 eggs
4 tablespoons grated Parmesan cheese

Place the chicken pieces, veal, carrots, celery, parsley, leek, salt, pepper and cold water in a soup kettle. Bring to a rolling boil and skim off any froth that may gather. Turn heat back to simmer, cover, and cook for 3 hours. Then strain the soup, discarding the meat and vegetables; you have already extracted all of their good. After the broth has reached room temperature, place it in the coldest part of your refrigerator. Remove the solidified fat that forms on the top after chilling.

Put the broth back on the stove and bring to a rolling boil. Place the 4 slices of bread in the bottom of 4 ovenproof bowls. Break an egg over each slice of bread and sprinkle the egg with a tablespoon of the Parmesan cheese. Pour 1 cup of the boiling broth into each bowl. Put the bowls in a 350° F. oven for 10 minutes, or until the egg has become firm and white. Serve at once, piping hot. Serves 4.

Variation:

If you like tomato flavor in soup, add 2 very ripe tomatoes to the vegetables.

GOLDEN CHICKEN SOUP—JEWISH STYLE

It took me a long time to find out the secret of what our Jewish neighbor put into her soup to make it golden, rich and delicious. I tried and tried to imitate it, but my soup would always be a pale copy. On Friday nights her golden chicken soup would send everyone into ecstasies.

Finally, I pinned her down into letting me watch her make it. When she tossed in the chicken feet, I almost flipped. She insisted they made the soup, and sure enough they did.

It's hard to find a chicken with its feet intact on today's market. If you have a good Kosher butcher nearby, you are in luck. If you cannot find such a butcher, order your soup hen several days in advance with two pairs of chicken feet. Sometimes you'll get feet that the chicken in the pot never used for walking, but this makes little difference in the flavor of this delicious soup. There is some element in the cartilage and yellow coloring of the feet that gives this soup its enchanting flavor.

Here are the ingredients for wonderful chicken soup:

1 5-pound stewing hen, cut up
4 chicken feet
1 tablespoon salt
¼ teaspoon white pepper
12 cups cold water
3 medium-sized carrots, peeled but left whole
3 medium-sized onions, peeled but left whole
1 2- to 3-inch diameter celery root, peeled and cut into 1-inch pieces
2 parsnips, peeled and cut into quarters
1 6-inch-long zucchini squash, peeled and cut into ½-inch discs

If the chicken contain a lot of fat, remove it and save it for frying other foods. If you don't remove it you'll only have to skim it off later .

Singe the little feathers off the chicken feet over an open flame. Scrub the feet in lukewarm water with a stiff brush. Place the feet in scalding hot water for 15 minutes. Then peel away all the tough yellow skin. They are now ready for the soup.

Place the chicken pieces, chicken feet, salt, pepper and cold water in a soup kettle with a tight-fitting cover. Add the carrots, onions, celery root, parsnips and zucchini. Bring to a rolling boil and remove any froth that gathers on top.

Cover and cook over very low heat for 3 to 4 hours, or until the chicken is tender enough to fall away from the bones.

Strain the soup; save the pieces of chicken meat, but discard the vegetables. This is not wasteful, because all of their flavor is now in your delicious soup. This soup can be served as a clear broth with pieces of chicken meat or it can be further enhanced with the addition of any of the following noodles or dumplings. Serves 6 generously.

MATZOH DUMPLINGS FOR GOLDEN CHICKEN SOUP

1 cup matzohs, broken up into 1-inch pieces
½ cup hot chicken broth
½ cup onion, chopped fine
3 tablespoons peanut oil
½ teaspoon salt
¼ teaspoon pepper
¼ teaspoon nutmeg, freshly grated
1 tablespoon parsley, chopped fine
2 tablespoons almond meal (available in most Kosher specialty sections of your market)
4 eggs, beaten until lemon yellow
1 cup matzoh meal (available in Kosher specialty section of your market)

Pour the hot chicken broth over the matzohs and allow them to soak and swell up. Push the matzohs pieces down into the broth from time to time so that they are evenly soaked.

Heat the peanut oil in a skillet, add the onion and sauté until the onion is glazed. Set aside to cool.

Place the moistened matzohs in a mixing bowl and, using a slotted spoon, beat them slightly. Add the cooled onion and oil, salt, pepper, nutmeg, parsley and almond meal. Stir and mix well. Add the beaten eggs and stir until all is well mixed. Gradually add the matzoh meal until the mixture is stiff enough to form into 1-inch diameter balls. Set the balls on a clean towel for about 1½ hours to permit the outsides to get slightly hard and dry; then drop into rapidly boiling soup. Cover and reduce heat to simmer; cook for 35 minutes. Do not uncover during this time. .

NOODLES FOR GOLDEN CHICKEN SOUP

2 cups all-purpose flour
4 large eggs
2 tablespoons ice water

Sift the flour twice. On the last sifting, let it form into a mound in the center of a mixing bowl. Make a hollow in the center of this flour mound. Break the eggs into this indentation and add the ice water. Start stirring from the middle; then, after slightly mixed, begin to knead until you have a uniform stiff, golden-colored dough. Divide the dough in half.

Place the dough on a floured board or pastry cloth and roll out until it is about 1/16 of an inch thick. This will give you two sheets of dough. Place the sheets of dough on a towel and allow to dry for a half hour.

Fold each sheet of dough into three or four thicknesses and cut into the desired size of noodle with a very sharp knife. Spread out the cut noodles to dry for another 30 minutes, then drop into rapidly boiling soup. Cook until the noodles are tender enough to break against the side of the kettle with a spoon or fork.

GOLDEN DOUGH BITS OR FARFEL FOR GOLDEN CHICKEN SOUP

1¼ cups all-purpose flour
2 large eggs, slightly beaten
1 brimming tablespoon ice water
½ teaspoon salt

Sift the flour twice, then add the eggs, water and salt. Knead until it can be formed into a ball. Let this ball of dough dry for about 30 to 35 minutes. If it is a muggy day, turn your oven to 250° F. for about 8 minutes, turn off, and place the dough ball in it to dry out. When the dough ball is hardened on the outside, grate over a coarse grater. Spread out the dough bits of a clean towel to dry completely. When dry, drop into rapidly boiling chicken broth. The farfel will sink to the bottom and then rise to the center of the soup when it is done.

PUFFY SQUARES FOR GOLDEN CHICKEN SOUP

4 teaspoons peanut oil
4 eggs, beaten until lemon yellow
1 cup all-purpose flour
1 teaspoon salt
1 teaspoon baking powder
Vegetable oil for deep frying

Stir the peanut oil into the beaten eggs. Sift the flour, salt and baking powder together three times. Gradually add the flour to the egg-oil mixture and form into a dough. Place on a floured board and pat out until it is in an oblong strip about ½ inch thick.

Using a sharp knife, cut the dough into ½-inch squares. Heat the vegetable oil to 350° F. Drop the squares a few at a time into the hot oil and fry until they are golden brown. Remove from the oil to paper toweling to permit them to drain.

Drop the fried squares into rapidly boiling hot broth, cover, and cook for 8 to 10 minutes, or until the puffs swell up in the soup. Serve at once.

MEAT DUMPLINGS FOR GOLDEN CHICKEN SOUP

1 cup ground beef
1 egg yolk
½ teaspoon salt
⅛ teaspoon nutmeg
2 slices white bread with crusts removed
½ cup lukewarm water
½ cup beef bone marrow, raw (your butcher can supply this)
½ cup dry bread crumbs

Mix the beef, egg yolk, salt and nutmeg together. Soak the white bread in the water. Chop up the raw marrow and place it in a skillet over low heat. Cook until it is somewhat melted and begins to brown a little. Remove from the heat.

Squeeze out the bread; add it to the meat along with the cooked beef marrow. Mix all well, then add the bread crumbs a little at a time until the mixture is stiff enough to form into balls about 1 inch in diameter. You might have to use a few additional bread crumbs, for beef marrow varies in its fat content. Drop the 1-inch balls into boiling chicken broth; cover and cook for 14 minutes without removing cover. Serve at once, piping hot.

CHICKEN BOOYAH

1 6-pound stewing chicken, cut up
1 pound veal from the leg
1 pound oxtail joints or 1 pound beef bone, cracked up
12 cups cold water
1 teaspoon salt
10 peppercorns
1 cup diced carrots
1 cup diced celery
½ cup diced green pepper
1 cup diced raw potato
1 cup shredded cabbage
1 10-ounce package frozen peas
1 10-ounce package frozen wax beans
½ cup parsley, chopped fine
¾ cup instant packaged rice
3 tablespoons instant chicken bouillon

Place the veal, oxtail, cold water, salt and peppercorns in a soup kettle and bring to a rolling boil. Skim off any froth that may gather; turn heat down to simmer and cook for 1½ hours. Now add the chicken pieces and again bring the soup to a rolling boil, skimming off any froth that may gather. Turn back to simmer and cook for another 1½ hours.

Add the carrots, celery, green pepper, potato, cabbage, peas and beans and cook for 30 minutes. Add the parsley, rice and bouillon and cook for an additional 30 minutes. Serve piping hot with saltine crackers.

Variations:

Add 2 medium-sized tomatoes at the same time as you add the cabbage, if you like a tomato flavor in chicken soup.

CHICKEN GUMBO

1 3- to 5-pound stewing chicken, cut into portion-sized pieces
1 cup diced lean ham
2 tablespoons butter
½ cup diced onion
¼ cup chopped parsley
⅛ teaspoon thyme
8 cups boiling water
1 cup sliced okra (available in the frozen food section of your
    supermarket)
1 bay leaf
½ teaspoon salt
¼ teaspoon pepper
1 quart stewing oysters with their liquid
1 cup raw shelled deveined shrimp, cut into 1-inch pieces
2 cups hot cooked fluffy rice

Place the chicken, ham and butter in a large soup kettle
and sauté until the chicken is golden brown. Be sure to place
any fat sides of the chicken pieces on the hot surface of the
pan to render down the fat, which will aid the browning. If
the chicken is lean and without any fat, use additional butter
for browning. Add the onion, parsley and thyme, and continue
to sauté until the onion becomes transparent. Add the boiling
water, okra, bay leaf, salt and pepper and bring to a rolling
boil. Skim off any froth that appears. Turn heat down to
simmer and cook for 55 minutes, or until the chicken can be
pierced with a fork.

Add the oysters, their liquid and the shrimp. Cook for 10
minutes longer, or until the shrimp turns pink and the oyster
edges curl. Place ½ cup cooked rice in each soup bowl and
cover with the gumbo, making sure that each bowl has a portion of chicken, oysters and shrimp.

CHICKEN-VEGETABLE SOUP

1 4-pound stewing chicken, cut up
12 cups cold water
1 cup diced raw carrots
1 cup diced parsley root
1 cup diced onion
1 cup chopped cabbage
½ cup chopped celery
½ cup canned drained tomatoes
½ cup diced kohlrabi
1 tablespoon salt
¼ teaspoon black pepper

Place the chicken and cold water in a soup kettle. Bring to a rolling boil and remove any froth that gathers on top.

Add all the vegetables, salt and pepper, and after the soup again reaches a rolling boil, skim once more if necessary; then reduce the heat to simmer. Cover and cook for 2 to 3 hours, or until the chicken is tender and can be pulled apart with a fork. Remove the chicken from the soup. Remove all the meat from the bones. Discard the skin and bones and return the meat to the soup.

Serve piping hot with saltines. Serves 6.

Chapter VI

CHICKEN SANDWICHES

WHEN I WAS a youngster a trip on a train meant only one thing to me. I could go into the diner with my folks and order a chicken sandwich. When that sandwich arrived, with lettuce and two thick slices of white meat topped with mayonnaise, I felt that this was the top of the world. No matter how my mother tried, she could never make a sandwich that I would agree was as good as the one I had on the train.

It was not until many years later that I found out the secret of those sandwiches. They did not contain ordinary chicken like we had at home; it was capon. The cooks roasted the capons with stuffing for one item on the menu, and saved the breasts for sandwiches. During the summer months, when appetites require less hearty food, the capons were roasted without the stuffing and used primarily for sandwiches and salads. To top that, when the capons were roasted for summer use they were not actually roasted crispy brown, as one pictures it when the magic phrase "roast chicken" is used, but rather they were steam-roasted. The capons were prepared in a roaster with a very tight-fitting cover, with salt, pepper and a little water. This was in the days before aluminum foil wrapping, too.

Now, I am not saying that the only way to make a good chicken sandwich is to use capon. But if you are going to serve a lot of chicken sandwiches and you want them to delight the eaters, capon is your best bet. As mentioned previously, capon is a rooster with its sex privileges removed. As a result of this denial of nature's urge, these chickens develop large meaty breasts and are super tender. This is not a hard and fast rule in capons, for I've met a couple in my cooking experiences who must have fruitlessly chased hens anyway; they were as tough as nails. For the most part, however, capons are pretty tender birds.

The ordinary roasting chicken one finds in the market is good sandwich material too. However, the breast portion is not as full nor as tender as that of capon.

The best rule I have for good chicken sandwiches is to

devote the chicken to it. Do not boil all the flavor out of a chicken for soup and then use the tasteless fibers that are left for sandwiches. They will be just pale imitations of what a good chicken sandwich should be. One would not boil a beef roast for hours to make broth and then slice the meat for sandwiches. The same holds true for chicken.

To steam-roast a chicken or capon for sandwiches, simply salt and pepper the bird inside and out; wrap it tightly in aluminum foil and place it in a 325° F. oven, allowing 45 minutes to the pound. Cooking time, as always, depends on the tenderness of the bird. Always test the thickest portions with a sharp fork before pronouncing it done.

Chicken or capon can be roasted for sandwiches the day before you need it. When you do this, let the bird cool to room temperature and then place it in the coldest part of your refrigerator. Wrap the bird lightly in aluminum foil or place it in a covered dish before putting it away.

Chicken sandwiches of the well-known type—you know, slices of succulent chicken, lettuce, mayonnaise and fresh bread—will not be covered in this chapter because most people know how to put these together quite expertly.

We are going to deal with chicken sandwiches that are unique and different in flavor. Many of the recipes call for chopped or minced chicken; despite this, the chicken should be cooked primarily for sandwiches even when it is chopped. However, there is no reason why leftover chicken cannot be used, provided the flavors from the original cooking do not conflict with those of the new ingredients you are mixing for the sandwich.

CHICKEN BURGERS SUPREME

4 tomatoes, about 3 inches in diameter, very firm and not overripe
2 cups cooked, chopped chicken, both white and dark meat
½ cup onion, chopped fine
1 tablespoon melted margarine or butter
2 tablespoons soft white bread crumbs
2 tablespoons parsley, chopped fine
2 eggs, beaten until lemon yellow
⅛ teaspoon cinnamon
½ teaspoon salt
¼ teaspoon pepper

Dipping mix:

1 egg, beaten until lemon yellow, plus 1 tablespoon water
½ cup flour
¼ teaspoon salt
3 tablespoons margarine (for frying)
4 hamburger buns

Peel the tomatoes by dipping them in scalding water.
Remove the stem end. Cut the tomatoes in half and scoop
out the pulp, leaving about a ½-inch wall. Place the pulp
in a mixing bowl along with the chicken, onion, margarine,
bread crumbs, parsley, eggs, cinnamon, salt and pepper. Mix
thoroughly.

Fill each tomato half with the stuffing. Press it in well
and form into a flat patty on the open end. Mix the egg and
water thoroughly. Dip each stuffed tomato into the egg mixture. Mix the flour and salt and dip the tomatoes into it. Melt
the margarine in a large skillet and fry the patties, meat side
down, until they are golden brown.

Toast the hamburger buns under the broiler, and place
each patty, meat side down, on one half of a toasted hamburger bun. Place in a 475° F. oven for 5 to 8 minutes, or
until the tomato begins to soften and get bubbly. Serve at
once, piping hot. Serves 8.

Variations:

To be really festive, cut off the rounded dome end of each
    tomato so that you have a flat surface after they have been
    stuffed and sautéed. Place a tablespoon of grated cheddar,
    American or Swiss cheese on this flat surface before you
    put the sandwiches in a 475° F. oven. Bake until the cheese
    has melted.
Add ½ cup chopped toasted almonds to the stuffing mix-
    ture.
Add ½ cup chopped toasted pecans to the stuffing mixture.
Add 2 tablespoons of green pepper, chopped fine, to the
    stuffing mixture if you like pepper flavor.
If you would like to use these stuffed tomatoes as a main
    meat course dish, eliminate the hamburger buns and place
    the sautéed tomatoes, meat side down, in a baking dish;
    add three tablespoons water, cover and bake in a 400° F.
    oven for 25 minutes.

CHICKEN HASH PATTIES IN BUNS

2 cups cooked chopped chicken meat, light and dark
2 cups boiled potatoes, chopped fine
¼ cup parsley, chopped fine
¼ cup sweet onion, chopped fine
¼ cup green pepper, chopped fine
¼ cup boiling water with 1 tablespoon instant chicken bouillon dissolved in it
2 eggs, beaten until lemon yellow
¾ cup fine bread crumbs
3 tablespoons margarine
8 hamburger buns, slightly heated in the oven

Mix the chicken and the chopped potatoes together. Add the parsley, onion, green pepper and water with bouillon. Mix all very well. Add the beaten eggs and mix again. Form into eight patties; dip them in the bread crumbs so they are coated on all sides. Melt the margarine in a skillet over low heat and sauté the patties until they are golden brown on each side. Place a patty in each of the hamburger buns and serve piping hot. Serves 8.

This is an excellent stretcher recipe that seems to please the teenage group because they get enough to eat as well as a variation of flavors. These patties can also be made up into croquette shape and fried in deep fat. Garnished with creamed peas or creamed mushrooms they make a tremendous hit.

HOT CHICKEN AND VEAL LOAF SANDWICHES

2 cups cooked chopped chicken, both light and dark meat
6 slices veal loaf luncheon meat, ⅛ inch thick, diced into ¼-inch squares
1 tablespoon grated onion
1 tablespoon parsley, chopped fine
2 hard-boiled eggs, chopped fine
½ cup mayonnaise
8 hamburger buns

Mix the chicken, veal loaf, grated onion, parsley, eggs and mayonnaise together until all is blended and well-mixed. Place a mound of the mixture in the center of each bun bottom. Replace the bun tops and wrap in squares of aluminum foil. Place buns in a 375° F. oven for 15 minutes. Serve at once, piping hot. Serves 8.

CHICKEN LOAF FOR RYE BREAD SANDWICHES

2 cups cooked chicken meat, both light and dark
½ teaspoon salt
¼ teaspoon pepper
¼ teaspoon pulverized sage
¼ teaspoon marjoram
1 tablespoon wine vinegar
1 teaspoon yellow prepared mustard
1 tablespoon parsley, chopped fine
¼ cup hot water with 1 tablespoon instant chicken bouillon
dissolved in it

Put the chicken meat through the food chopper, using the coarse blade. After chopping, add the salt, pepper, sage and marjoram and mix very thoroughly.

Add the vinegar, mustard and chopped parsley to the hot water with the bouillon in it. Add this mixture to the chopped chicken and blend all very well.

Place the mixture in the bottom of a loaf pan. Using another loaf pan as a cover, press the bottom of the second loaf pan on the chicken. Bear down with a lot of weight. Tilt the pan to drain off any excess liquid that may gather. Tie the two pans together tightly so that there is constant pressure on top of the chicken. Place in the refrigerator overnight. Unmold onto a platter garnished with lettuce or endive. Cut into thin slices and place on pieces of rye bread. Serve open-faced. Makes 16 generous sandwiches on snack type rye bread.

CHICKEN 'N CHEESE BURGERS

2 cups cooked diced chicken meat, both light and dark
1 cup mild American cheese cut in ¼-inch cubes
½ cup green pepper, chopped fine
½ teaspoon salt
¼ teaspoon pepper
8 hamburger buns
Aluminum foil

Mix the chicken, cheese, green pepper, salt and pepper together. Place a generous spoonful of the mixture in the center of each hamburger bun. Replace bun tops and then wrap each bun in a square of aluminum foil. Place in a 375° F. oven for 15 minutes. Serve at once, piping hot. Garnish with dill pickles.

HOT CHICKEN SANDWICHES SUPREME

4 slices chicken white meat 3 x 3 x ½ inches, or 1 cup
    thinly sliced chicken white meat of various sizes
2 English muffins, split in half and lightly brushed with
    melted butter or margarine
1 10-ounce can cream of chicken soup
1 teaspoon instant chicken bouillon
½ cup slivered toasted almonds
1 tablespoon parsley, chopped fine

Place the English muffin halves under the broiler for a few
seconds until they are golden brown. (If your toaster is wide
enough to take muffins, they can be toasted in this manner
and buttered later.)

Place the toasted muffin halves on individual ovenproof
serving dishes or an ovenproof platter. Put a portion of the
sliced chicken meat over the cut-open side of each muffin.

Pour the soup into a double boiler over rapidly boiling
water. When heated through, stir in the granules of chicken
bouillon.

Pour generous spoonsful of the hot chicken soup over the
muffins topped with the chicken. Sprinkle each with the toasted
almonds and a bit of the parsley.

Place in a 475° F. oven for 5 minutes, or until the soup
begins to bubble and brown slightly. Serve at once. Serves 4.

CHICKEN AND JELLIED TONGUE SANDWICHES

2 cups cooked chopped chicken, both light and dark meat
1 cup diced jellied tongue cut in ¼-inch cubes
¼ cup diced green pepper
2 tablespoons India pickle relish, drained
1 tablespoon capers, chopped fine
½ cup mayonnaise
12 slices rye bread with caraway seeds, spread with margarine
6 lettuce leaves

Mix the chicken, tongue, green pepper, India relish, capers
and mayonnaise together until well-blended. Spread the mixture ¼ inch thick over six slices of bread. Place a lettuce leaf
on top of this and follow with another slice of rye. Press the
sandwiches together, then cut diagonally into four pieces.
Serves 6.

WHITE CHICKEN MEAT AND OLIVE SANDWICHES

1 cup cooked chicken white meat, chopped very fine
¼ cup celery, chopped fine
3 tablespoons chopped ripe olives
½ cup mayonnaise
1 teaspoon lemon juice
½ teaspoon salt
¼ teaspoon pepper
4 slices whole wheat bread (you may lightly butter the bread)
8 to 10 leafy sprigs of water cress
8 ripe olives
8 pickled sweet cherry peppers

Mix the chicken, celery, olives, mayonnaise, lemon juice, salt and pepper together. Work into a blend of spreading consistency.

Spread each of the 8 pieces of bread with about ¼ inch of the mixture. Press two sprigs of water cress into the spread on one of the pieces of bread and cover with the other piece. Cut into quarters and place on a plate with 2 ripe olives and 2 cherry peppers. Makes 4 generous sandwiches.

Variations:

Use chopped pimiento-stuffed olives in place of the ripe olives for a more distinct olive flavor.
Use the green leaves from iceberg lettuce in place of the water cress.
Use enriched white bread in place of the whole wheat bread.

CHICKEN AND CHIVES SANDWICHES

2 cups cooked chicken, chopped fine
1 tablespoon grated sweet onion
¼ cup chives, cut fine
½ cup mayonnaise
3 hard-boiled egg yolks, chopped fine

Mix all of the ingredients together until they are of spreadable consistency. Spread on pieces of enriched white bread that have been lightly toasted, cover with another slice of toast and cut into quarters.

Make 8 generous sandwiches.

CHICKEN AND WALNUT SANDWICHES

2 cups cooked chicken white meat, chopped fine
1 cup English walnuts
1 tablespoon peanut oil
½ cup celery, chopped fine
½ cup mayonnaise
½ teaspoon salt
¼ teaspoon pepper

Place the walnuts in a saucepan, cover with water and bring to a rolling boil for 3 minutes. Cool below running water and remove the walnut skins. They will come off easily in this method of blanching. Drain the blanched walnuts on paper toweling.

Place the peanut oil in a skillet over low heat. When hot, add the walnuts. Sauté the walnuts until they just begin to turn golden, then remove from the heat at once. Chop the walnuts to about the same consistency as the chicken.

Mix the chicken and walnuts together. Add the celery, mayonnaise, salt and pepper and blend until the mixture is of spreading consistency. Spread on pieces of enriched white bread. Makes 12 generous sandwiches.

Chicken and walnut spread lends itself well to open-faced sandwiches. You can use either white or whole wheat bread or cocktail crackers. Garnish each with a sprig of parsley.

CHICKEN, HAM AND EGG SANDWICHES

1 cup cooked chicken, chopped fine, light and dark meat
1 cup lean ground ham
¼ cup melted butter or margarine
¼ teaspoon prepared mustard
4 hard-boiled eggs, peeled and chopped fine
1 tablespoon lemon juice
½ teaspoon salt
¼ teaspoon pepper
2 tablespoons mayonnaise
1 tablespoon parsley, chopped fine
10 stuffed olives

Mix the chicken and ham together. Add the butter, mustard, eggs, lemon juice, salt, pepper, mayonnaise and parsley. Mix well until it is of spreadable consistency.

Spread on slices of snack type rye bread and garnish each with a half of stuffed olive. Makes approximately 20 sandwiches.

Variation:

Omit the ham and use 2 cups of chopped chicken meat.

CHICKEN LIVER SANDWICH SPREAD

1 pound chicken livers
1 cup onions, chopped fine
3 tablespoons chicken fat or margarine (chicken fat is better)
4 hard-boiled eggs, peeled and quartered
½ teaspoon seasoned pepper (available in the spice section of most supermarkets)
½ teaspoon salt

Sauté the chicken livers and onions in the chicken fat until the livers are tender enough to cut with the side of a fork. Remove from heat and allow to cool.

Put the livers and onions through a food chopper; follow this with the quarters of hard-boiled eggs. Add the pepper and salt. Then put the whole mixture through the food chopper once more so that it is of fine, spreadable consistency. Place in the refrigerator about an hour before using so that it firms up.

Spread on both sides of slices of wheat bread, then place a lettuce leaf between the two pieces of bread.

This can also be used as an appetizer by spreading on Melba toast or rounds of white bread that have been toasted under the broiler. Garnish the rounds with a bit of crumbled cooked egg yolk and a dash of paprika for color.

JELLIED CHICKEN LOAF FOR SANDWICHES

2 cups chicken white meat, chopped very fine or put through
   the coarse blade of the food chopper
¾ cup boiling water with 1 tablespoon instant chicken bouillon dissolved in it
2 tablespoons unflavored gelatin
½ teaspoon salt
¼ teaspoon pepper
2 tablespoons grated horseradish
1 cup whipping cream, whipped until it stands in peaks
½ cup canned pimiento, chopped fine
4 rings green pepper, sliced ⅛ inch thick

Place the boiling water and chicken bouillon in the top of
a double boiler over rapidly boiling water. Sprinkle in the
gelatin, a little at a time; stir constantly until all of the
gelatin is dissolved. Add the salt, pepper and horseradish.
Mix well, then add the chicken meat. Set aside to cool.

When cool, fold in the whipped cream and the bits of
pimiento. Lay the four rings of green pepper in the bottom
of a loaf pan and pour the mixture of chicken and gelatin
over the top. Place in the coldest part of the refrigerator for
6 hours or overnight. Unmold on a platter garnished with
endive or lettuce. Cut in thin slices and place between buttered
pieces of enriched white bread. Makes 8 generous sandwiches.

Variations:

Thicker slices of this loaf can also be served on lettuce as a
   hearty meat salad. Use French dressing as a garnish.

CHICKEN AND PARMESAN SANDWICHES

1 cup chicken, chopped very fine; either light or dark meat
1 tablespoon Parmesan cheese
¼ cup dairy sour cream
¼ teaspoon prepared yellow mustard
½ teaspoon salt
¼ teaspoon pepper
1 tablespoon chili sauce
1 tablespoon mayonnaise
8 slices white enriched bread, lightly buttered
4 green outside leaves of lettuce, iceberg type
8 strips of green pepper, ½ inch x 1½ inches
8 ripe olives

Mix the chicken, cheese and sour cream together until all is a smooth paste. Add the mustard, salt, pepper, chili sauce and mayonnaise and again mix until all is smoothly blended to spreading consistency.

Spread each of the slices of white bread with a ¼-inch thick layer of the chicken mixture. Place a piece of lettuce on each of four slices, and press the other slice of bread over the lettuce. Cut into four wedges. Place on a plate with 2 strips of the green pepper and two of the olives for a garnish. Makes 4 generous sandwiches.

Variations:

Use tender pieces of leafy water cress in place of the lettuce, for a different flavor
Use bib lettuce in place of iceberg lettuce for a different flavor

Chapter VII

INTERNATIONAL CHICKEN RECIPES

COOKS THE WORLD over have been inventing fabulous ways to serve chicken since time immemorial. This chapter contains some of our favorites that definitely have a foreign accent.

Since most of these recipes for chicken come from regions where the laying hen was more important than tomorrow's dinner, you will find that you can use the economical stewing hens that grace our supermarket counters. A chicken is not used for food in most foreign lands until her egg production has gone way down. You will find that these recipes call for a longer cooking time than some of the others.

When picking out a stewing hen, you can usually tell the degree of tenderness by pressing the breastbone. If this bone is rigid and does not have much flex—beware, this bird is a tough old veteran of the barnyard. These tough ones are only good for soup.

With today's controlled growing of chicken for food, there is little chance of your getting a bird so tough that it is not edible. However, it is always wise and economical to shop carefully when buying chicken.

MEXICAN CHICKEN BAKE

3 cups diced, cooked chicken, both light and dark meat
¾ cup diced red Italian onions
½ cup diced green pepper
2 10-ounce cans cream of mushroom soup
3 drops Tabasco (more if you like it hot)
2 cups corn chips or broken up fried tacos
1½ cups grated mild Cheddar cheese

Mix the chicken, onions, green pepper, soup and Tabasco. Fold in the corn chips. Place in a shallow baking pan about 9″ x 12″ in size. Spread the grated cheese over the top.

Place in a 350° F. oven for 25 minutes, or until the cheese is melted and has started to turn golden brown.

Serve at once, piping hot. Serves 6.

Variations:

Use grated American cheese in place of the Cheddar cheese.
Add 1 10-ounce package of frozen black-eyed peas.
Add 1 #2 can of drained pinto beans.
Add 1 #2 can of drained chick peas.
Add 1 10-ounce package of frozen green peas.

MEXICAN CHICKEN

1 3- to 4-pound frying chicken, cut up into portion-sized pieces
¼ cup cooking oil (olive or peanut oil, for instance)
1 pound pork steak cut into 1-inch pieces
4 breakfast pork sausages, cut into 1-inch pieces
¾ cup chopped onion
2 cloves garlic, chopped fine
1 cup tomato sauce
1 teaspoon paprika
1 #2 can chicken broth
1 cup raw, shelled, deveined shrimp, cut into 1-inch pieces
1 7½ ounce can minced clams, juice and all
3 large canned pimientos cut into ¼-inch pieces
2 tablespoons chopped parsley
1 cup packaged instant rice
½ teaspoon salt
¼ teaspoon pepper

Sauté the chicken in the cooking oil until it is golden brown. Remove the chicken and set aside. Sauté the pork steak and sausages in the oil until browned. Remove from oil and set aside. Sauté the onion and garlic in the remaining oil until the onion is soft and tender. Pour off the excess oil. Add the tomato sauce, paprika, chicken broth and shrimp. Simmer until the shrimp is pink and firm. Add the clams, chicken, pork and sausage and cook for 20 minutes over low heat. Stir in the pimiento, parsley, rice, salt and pepper, cover and cook for 15 minutes longer, or until the rice is tender and fluffy.

Serve piping hot. Serves 6.

MEXICAN CHICKEN ROAST

Mexican roast chicken is delicious. The secret of the flavor is that while roasting, the chicken is sealed so that none of the steam can escape. In Mexico, the chicken is baked in an earthen pot with a tight-fitting cover that is sealed with moist clay. When the chicken is done the clay is easily removed because the oven heat does not harden it to pottery consistency. Since few of us have a handy clay bank on which to draw, we use flour and water as a seal around the edge of the dish. This is messy to clean up and to get off the rim of the baking dish; however, the reward in flavor is well worth it.

1 4-pound roasting chicken
¼ cup French brandy or Cognac
½ teaspoon salt
½ teaspoon Accent
¼ teaspoon pepper
1 2-ounce can of pâté de foie gras (available in the gourmet food section of your supermarket)
3 tablespoons water mixed with 2 tablespoons flour (for paste-seal method)

Dry the chicken thoroughly with a clean dish towel. Using a pastry brush, coat the chicken inside and out with the brandy. If you have any brandy left, pour it inside the chicken. Sprinkle the chicken inside and out with the salt, Accent and pepper. Spread the pâté de foie gras over the breast and legs of the chicken.

Place the chicken in a large casserole with a tight-fitting cover. Seal the edge of the cover with the paste made from the flour and water. Place in a 400° F. oven for 1 hour. Remove the paste seal with a sharp knife. If you do not care to use this paste-seal method, you can fasten the cover tightly with a length of wire or by placing a heavy ovenproof skillet over the top as a weight. Caution should be taken when opening the roasting dish because there will be steam gathered inside. Always open it away from you. Allow the roasting pan to cool for 5 minutes or so before opening; this will reduce the amount of steam.

The chicken can also be roasted in a tightly sealed wrapping of heavy aluminum foil. If you use this method, pierce the foil in several places with a sharp fork after the chicken is baked to allow the steam to escape. Serves 4.

ARROZ CON POLLO
(Mexican Stewed Chicken with Rice)

1 3-pound fryer, cut up into portion-sized pieces
¼ cup cooking oil
½ cup chopped onion
1 clove garlic, sliced paper thin
½ cup chopped green pepper
1 #2 can tomatoes
½ teaspoon salt
¼ teaspoon pepper
½ teaspoon paprika
4 cloves
2 small bay leaves
1 cup raw rice
1 10-ounce package frozen peas, thawed to room temperature
1 sweet red pepper, cut into ¼-inch pieces (optional)

Dry the pieces of chicken with paper toweling. Place the oil in a large skillet and sauté the chicken until golden brown. Add the onion, garlic and green pepper and sauté until the onion is transparent and glazed. Then add the tomatoes, salt, pepper, paprika, cloves and bay leaves. Bring to a rolling boil, and then turn the heat back to simmer. Cover and simmer for 25 minutes. Add the rice; stir it in well. Cover and simmer for 20 minutes longer, or until the grains of rice are tender. Sprinkle the peas and pepper over the top, and cook, uncovered, for 5 minutes more. Serves 6. If you wish, remove the cloves and bay leaves before serving.

Variations:

Use 3 pounds of chicken legs only instead of the whole chicken.

If you wish to use a stewing hen for this dish, you may. However the cooking time after the addition of the tomatoes should be increased until the thickest portions of the hen can be pierced with a fork.

SPANISH CHICKEN

1 5-pound stewing chicken, cut into portion-sized pieces
¼ cup butter
3 medium-sized fresh tomatoes, cut into ¼-inch slices, or
   1 #2 can of tomatoes, drained (save the juice)
¾ cup chopped onion
¾ cup chopped green pepper
¼ teaspoon orégano
¼ teaspoon ground cloves
1 teaspoon salt
¼ teaspoon pepper
1 teaspoon Accent
1½ cups raw rice
2½ cups tomato juice
1 2-ounce can chopped ripe olives
1 package frozen green peas, thawed

Melt the butter in a large skillet, then place the chicken in the skillet over moderate heat. Sauté until all sides are evenly browned. Pour off any remaining butter and reserve it.

Add the tomatoes, onion, green pepper, orégano, cloves, salt, pepper and Accent. Simmer for 8 minutes, turning each piece of chicken during this time. Then place the chicken and vegetables in a casserole or baking dish.

Return the reserved butter to the skillet and brown the raw rice in it. Add the tomato juice and olives. Stir well and pour over the chicken. Place in a 350° F. oven for 1 hour. Then spread the peas over the top of the casserole and return to the oven for an additional 30 minutes. Serve piping hot. Serves 6.

CHICKEN CASTILLANE

This is a dish of Spanish origin that was brought to Mexico during the conquest. It is a real treat, both to the eye and the taste buds.

1 3-pound fryer, cut up for easy boning
2 cups cold water
½ teaspoon salt
¼ teaspoon pepper

Sauce:

2 tablespoons butter
1½ cups onion, cut into ¼-inch cubes
¾ cup green pepper, cut into ¼-inch cubes
2 cloves garlic, sliced paper thin
¼ cup chopped parsley
3 medium-sized tomatoes, peeled and cut into eighths, or 1
    #2 can tomatoes, drained
1 cup dry white wine
¼ cup seedless raisins
3 cups hot fluffy boiled rice
1 pimiento, cut into ¼-cubes

Place the chicken pieces, water, salt and pepper in a sauce-pan and bring to a rolling boil. Skim off any froth that gathers on top. Reduce the heat to a simmer and cook for 30 minutes, or until the chicken can be pierced with a fork at the thickest parts. Remove the chicken from the broth and set aside to cool. When cool, remove all the meat from the bones and cut it up into bite-sized pieces. Save the broth until later.

Melt the butter in a large deep skillet; add the onion and green pepper; sauté over low heat until the onion is transparent and glazed. Add the garlic, parsley, tomatoes, wine, raisins, chicken and 2 cups of chicken broth.

If you do not have two cups of broth, add water. Cook, uncovered, for 15 minutes over low heat.

Should you prefer a thicker sauce, mix 2 tablespoons corn-starch in ½ cup water and stir this into the sauce. Cook over low heat, stirring constantly, until the sauce is thickened and rather transparent.

Mound the hot rice in the middle of a deep platter and pour the chicken and sauce over it. Sprinkle the pimiento over the top. Serve at once, piping hot. Serves 4.

Variations:

Add ¾ cup coarsely chopped toasted pecans 5 minutes before
    serving.
Add ½ cup diced sweet red peppers along with the green
    peppers.
Serve over broad, boiled egg noodles instead of rice.
Use 2 cups of wild rice and 1 cup of domestic rice.
Sprinkle ½ cup crisp fried bacon cubes over the top along
    with the pimiento, for added flavor.

CHICKEN CACCIATORE #1

2 2-pound broilers, cut up into portion-sized pieces
¼ cup butter
1 cup onions, chopped fine
1 cup green pepper, chopped fine
3 cloves garlic, chopped and minced
1 #2 can tomatoes
1 cup tomato sauce
1 cup dry red wine
1 teaspoon salt
¼ teaspoon pepper
3 bay leaves
½ teaspoon thyme, crushed

Melt the butter in a large skillet that has a tight-fitting cover. Brown the pieces of chicken evenly on all sides in the melted butter.

Add the onions, green pepper, garlic, tomatoes and tomato sauce. Mix well, then stir in the wine, salt and pepper. Add the bay leaves and thyme. Cover tightly and cook over low heat for 35 minutes. Turn the chicken pieces once during this cooking period. They are done if you can pierce the thickest portions with a fork.

This chicken is excellent served with cooked spaghetti or cooked broad egg noodles. Serves 4 to 6.

CHICKEN CACCIATORE #2

1 3- to 4-pound fryer, cut up into portion-sized pieces
½ cup olive oil
½ cup coarsely chopped onion
3 cloves garlic, sliced paper thin
1 3-ounce can tomato paste
1 cup water
1 #2 can Italian style tomatoes
1 cup mushroom stems and pieces
½ teaspoon orégano
½ teaspoon salt
¼ teaspoon pepper
1 teaspoon granulated sugar

Heat the olive oil in a large skillet and in it sauté the pieces of chicken until they are golden brown. Remove the chicken

78

from the oil and set aside. Cook the onion and garlic in the remaining hot olive oil until the onion is transparent. Drain off any excess oil. Add the tomato paste, water, tomatoes (juice and all), mushrooms, orégano, salt, pepper and sugar. Bring to a boil and cook for 5 minutes. Then add the chicken, cover, and cook for 30 minutes longer at simmer. Serve with boiled spaghetti or broad egg noodles. If desired, sprinkle with Parmesan cheese. Serves 4.

CHICKEN CACCIATORE #3

1 2- to 3-pound broiler, cut up into portion-sized pieces
½ cup all-purpose flour
½ cup peanut oil
¾ cup coarsely chopped onion
2 cloves garlic, chopped fine
½ teaspoon salt
¼ teaspoon pepper
1 8-ounce can tomato sauce
1 #2 can Italian style tomatoes
1 large bay leaf
¼ teaspoon sweet basil

Dry each piece of chicken on paper toweling. Then place the flour in a paper sack and shake each piece of chicken in the flour until thoroughly coated.

Heat the peanut oil in a large skillet. Place the chicken pieces, skin side down, in the hot oil and brown evenly on both sides. Add the onion, garlic, salt and pepper. Continue to cook over moderate heat until the onion is limp and glazed. Add the tomato sauce and tomatoes. Bring to a rolling boil, then turn the heat back to simmer. Add the bay leaf and basil. Cover and continue to simmer for 50 minutes, or until the thickest pieces of chicken can be pierced with a fork. If the sauce gets too thick, add a little water.

Serve with hot boiled spaghetti, elbow macaroni, hot fluffy rice or boiled broad egg noodles. Garnish with a sprinkle of parsley or with Parmesan cheese. Serves 4.

CHICKEN CACCIATORE #4

2 2- to 3-pound fryer-broilers, cut into portion-sized pieces
½ cup all-purpose flour
½ teaspoon salt
¼ teaspoon pepper
½ cup olive oil
2 cloves garlic, sliced paper thin
1 teaspoon pulverized rosemary
8 strips anchovy, chopped fine
½ cup wine vinegar or cider vinegar
1 cup Burgundy or Chianti wine
¼ cup tomato sauce
½ cup hot water with 1 tablespoon instant chicken bouillon
   dissolved in it

Wipe the pieces of chicken with paper toweling. Mix the flour, salt and pepper together well and sprinkle on all sides of the chicken pieces. Let stand for 15 minutes.

Heat the olive oil in a large skillet with a tight-fitting cover. Add the garlic and sauté until the garlic begins to brown, then remove the garlic and discard. Sauté the pieces of chicken in this oil until they are golden brown on all sides.

Mix together the rosemary, anchovies and vinegar. Add this to the sautéed chicken. Mix together the wine, tomato sauce and hot water with chicken bouillon. Add this to the chicken. Cover tightly and continue to simmer for 25 minutes, or until the thickest pieces of chicken can be pierced with a fork. Serve piping hot. Serves 6.

CHICKEN CACCIATORE #5

1 5-pound stewing hen, cut into portion-sized pieces
½ cup olive oil
½ cup onion, chopped fine
1 tablespoon parsley, chopped fine
¼ cup celery, chopped fine
2 cloves garlic, chopped fine
1 bay leaf
½ teaspoon pulverized rosemary
1 cup dry sauterne
¼ teaspoon black pepper
1 teaspoon salt
½ cup instant rice as it comes from the package
½ cup water

Wipe the pieces of chicken with paper toweling. Heat the olive oil in a skillet with a tight-fitting cover. Add the pieces of chicken and brown them well on all sides. Add the onion, parsley, celery, garlic, bay leaf, rosemary and wine. Lower heat to simmer. Stir well. Sprinkle in the pepper, salt and instant rice. Make sure that all of the rice is submerged in the liquid. Add the water, cover tightly, and cook at simmer for 1 hour, or until the thickest portions of chicken can be pierced with a fork. Serve piping hot. Serves 6.

Variations:

Add 1 #2 can Italian style tomatoes and eliminate the last
  ½ cup water.
Substitute Chablis wine for the sauterne for a different flavor.
Substitute Reisling wine for the sauterne for a different flavor.
If you have a dry, light champagne that has gone flat, you may
  use it in place of sauterne.

ITALIAN CHICKEN BAKE

2 2- to 3-pound broilers, cut up into quarters
1 teaspoon salt
¼ teaspoon pepper
¾ cup melted butter
½ teaspoon garlic powder
2 cups fine bread crumbs
¾ cup grated Parmesan cheese
3 tablespoons dehydrated parsley flakes
½ teaspoon crushed orégano
¼ teaspoon thyme
¼ teaspoon savory

Rub the outside of the chicken pieces with the salt and pepper. Set aside.

Stir the garlic powder into the melted butter and set aside while you prepare the bread crumb mixture.

Mix the bread crumbs, cheese, parsley flakes orégano, thyme and savory together until all are blended and completely mixed.

Brush each piece of chicken with the garlic-flavored butter; then dip the buttered chicken in the seasoned bread crumb-cheese mixture. Place the chicken pieces in a shallow baking pan; bake in a 350° F. oven for 45 minutes, or until golden brown and thick pieces can be pierced with a sharp fork. Serve piping hot. Serves 6.

ITALIAN CHICKEN WITH GOLDEN SAUCE

1 3- to 5-pound stewing chicken, cut into portion-sized pieces
¼ cup butter
2 tablespoons olive oil
1½ cups Chablis wine
½ cup lemon juice
4 eggs, beaten until lemon yellow
½ teaspoon salt
¼ teaspoon pepper
½ teaspoon Accent

Wipe the chicken pieces with paper toweling. Place the butter and the olive oil in a skillet with a tight-fitting cover. Sauté the chicken over low heat until it is golden brown. Turn heat down to simmer, cover and continue to cook for an additional 35 minutes.

Then add the wine, cover and simmer for an additional 10 minutes, or until the thickest pieces of chicken can be pierced with a fork. Stir in lemon juice. Add the salt, pepper and Accent to the beaten eggs. Stir about 4 tablespoons of the wine gravy from the skillet into the eggs, then add the eggs to the chicken in the skillet. Stir constantly; continue to cook over very low heat until the gravy has thickened. Remove from heat immediately. Serves 6.

Variations:

Serve with hot fluffy boiled rice.
Serve with thin cooked spaghetti.
Serve with plain boiled broccoli.
Serve with boiled green asparagus spears.

CHICKEN TETRAZZINI

1 4- to 6-pound stewing chicken
½ cup diced celery
½ cup diced onion
1 teaspoon salt
3 tablespoons all-purpose flour
Dash of cayenne pepper
1 cup sliced mushroom stems and pieces
1 egg, beaten until lemon yellow
¼ cup half and half cream
1 8-ounce package fine egg noodles
¼ cup grated Parmesan cheese

Cut the chicken into serving-sized pieces and place in a kettle with the celery. Add just enough water to barely cover the meat; cook, covered, for 1 to 1½ hours, or until a fork will easily pierce the thickest part of the breast. Drain off and strain the broth and place it in the refrigerator so that the fat will solidify and can be skimmed off.

Meanwhile, cut the skin and bones from the chicken and discard them. Cut the chicken into bite-sized pieces. Set aside.

Skim off from the broth two tablespoons of the chicken fat and put it in the top of a double boiler over boiling water. Stir in the flour; add the cayenne. Add 1 cup of broth and continue to cook over hot water until thickened.

Sauté the mushrooms in 2 tablespoons of the chicken fat until they begin to brown. Mix the egg and cream together and then stir 2 tablespoons of the thickened sauce into this mixture. Add the egg and cream to the thickened sauce. Stir well and continue to cook for 5 minutes longer. Add the sautéed mushrooms and the chicken to the thickened sauce. Turn the heat low enough just to keep the mixture warm.

Cook the egg noodles in the remaining chicken broth. You may add more water, if necessary, to get as much liquid as specified on the noodle package. When the noodles are tender, drain them and place them in a rather shallow buttered baking dish. Pour the chicken and mushroom mixture over the noodles. Sprinkle the Parmesan cheese over the top. Place about 6 inches below the broiler flame to brown the cheese. Serve immediately. Serves 4.

ITALIAN CHICKEN AND GREEN PEPPERS

2 2-pound broiler-fryer chickens, cut up into portion-sized pieces
1 cup all-purpose flour
½ teaspoon orégano, powdered fine
½ cup olive oil
½ cup coarsely chopped onion
1 clove garlic, chopped fine
1 #2 can Italian style tomatoes
5 3-inch diameter green peppers

Wipe the pieces of chicken with paper toweling. Place the flour and orégano in a paper sack. Shake up and down to mix well. Add the pieces of chicken three or four at a time, and shake up and down so that they are thoroughly coated with the flavored flour. Place the floured chicken on a piece of waxed paper for 15 minutes to allow the flour to become thoroughly adhered.

Heat the olive oil in a large skillet with a tight-fitting cover. Add the onion and garlic and sauté until the onion becomes transparent. Add the chicken pieces and sauté until browned on all sides. Add the tomatoes after the chicken has browned.

Wash the green peppers under cold running water; remove the stem and seeds. Cut into 1-inch squares and distribute over and around the chicken. Cover and reduce heat to simmer; cook for 40 minutes, or until the thickest portions of the chicken can be pierced with a fork. Season to taste with salt and pepper and serve. Serves 6.

RUMANIAN CHICKEN PANCAKES

2 chicken breasts, cut in half
1½ cups water
1 cup coarsely chopped onion
½ teaspoon salt
¼ teaspoon pepper
4 green skinned pears, about 3 inches in diameter at largest end—not too ripe
2 tablespoons all-purpose flour
5 eggs, beaten until lemon yellow

Place the chicken breasts, water, onion, salt and pepper in a saucepan with a tight-fitting cover. Bring to a rolling boil and skim off any froth that may gather. Cover, turn heat back to simmer and cook for 35 minutes, or until the thickest portion of the chicken can be pierced with a fork.

Peel and core the pears; cut them into ½-inch cubes and add them to the boiling chicken. Cook 8 minutes, or until the edges of the pears begin to get transparent. Remove the pears and chicken from the heat. Allow to cool.

Remove the meat from the ribcage and discard the skin and bones. Drain the pears and onion and add them to the chicken. Chop all very fine. Sprinkle the flour over the top, then add the beaten eggs. Mix all very well. Pour by spoonsful onto a hot griddle and fry as you would pancakes. Serve at once, piping hot. Serves 4.

Variations:

Serve with portions of applesauce to which you have added nutmeg so that it has a very distinctive nutmeg flavor.
Serve with horseradish.
Serve with orange marmalade.

EAST INDIAN CHICKEN DELIGHT

4 chicken breasts
1 #2 can chicken broth
4 tablespoons butter
½ teaspoon salt
¼ teaspoon black pepper
½ cup dry white wine
3 egg yolks
½ cup whipping cream (unwhipped)
1 cup uncooked instant rice
2 tablespoons butter
¾ cup light-colored raisins
½ teaspoon salt
½ cup coarsely chopped pecans

Using a very sharp knife, remove the white meat from the ribcage. Cut it into bite-sized portions. Place the bones and skin in a saucepan with the can of chicken broth; simmer slowly while you prepare the rest of the recipe. Skim off any froth that may gather.

Melt the 4 tablespoons butter in a skillet and sauté the chicken until it is golden brown. Add the salt, pepper and wine; continue to simmer for a few minutes.

Mix the egg yolks and cream. Stir a few spoonsful of the wine gravy from the skillet into the egg yolks and cream. Then add the egg and cream mixture to the skillet. Stir rapidly and constantly while you are adding it to prevent curdling. Do not boil, just keep over low heat until the mixture is warmed through.

Strain the chicken broth into another saucepan; discard the bones. Stir in the rice, 2 tablespoons butter, raisins and salt. Cover and simmer for 15 minutes. Add the chopped pecans and stir with a fork.

Place the rice around the edge of a deep platter; pour the chicken mixture into the middle. Serve piping hot. Serves 6.

Variations:

Substitute saffron-flavored rice for the rice mixture; cook according to the directions on the package.
Substitute chopped toasted almonds for the pecans for a different taste.
Omit the raisins if you do not care for their sweetness.

Substitute 1 #2 can of beef broth for the chicken broth if you want the rice to have a heartier flavor. In this case save the chicken bones for the next time you need chicken-flavored broth.

Substitute long-grain brown rice for the instant rice. Add ½ cup of water to the broth and cook until the brown rice is tender. Follow cooking directions on the package, as cooking time for brown rice varies with the brands used.

HAWAIIAN CHICKEN WITH COCONUT

2 chicken breasts, cut in half
2 cups cold water
½ teaspoon salt
¼ teaspoon pepper
¼ cup uncooked rice
½ cup water with 2 tablespoons cornstarch dissolved in it
2 tablespoons instant chicken bouillon
1 8-ounce can pineapple wedges, drained
1 8-ounce can mandarin orange sections, drained
¾ cup fried coconut chips (available in the gourmet section of food stores)
¼ cup parsley, chopped fine

Place the chicken breasts, water, salt, pepper and rice in a saucepan. Bring to a rolling boil and remove any froth that may gather. Turn the heat down to simmer, cover, and cook for 30 minutes, or until the breasts can be pierced with a sharp fork at the thickest part. Remove the breasts from the broth and allow them to cool.

Continue to let the broth simmer as you stir in the water and cornstarch mixture. Add the chicken bouillon and continue to simmer, stirring constantly, until the mixture has thickened. Add the pineapple wedges and orange sections and keep warm over very low heat.

Meanwhile, remove the white meat from the bones; try to remove each breast section in one piece. Place on an oven-proof platter; pour the broth and fruit over all. Mix the coconut chips and parsley and sprinkle over the top of the chicken in the thickened broth. Place the platter about 6 inches away from the broiler heat for 5 minutes, or until the coconut and chicken just begin to brown. Serve at once, piping hot. Serves 4.

TROPICAL CHICKEN WITH WINE

1 4- to 6-pound stewing chicken
½ teaspoon salt
1 teaspoon Accent
¼ teaspoon pepper
6 tablespoons all-purpose flour
6 tablespoons butter
¼ teaspoon grated nutmeg
¼ teaspoon ground cloves
¼ teaspoon ground cinnamon
1 13-ounce can pineapple chunks in extra heavy syrup
½ cup seedless raisins
¾ cup white wine such as Chablis
2 avocado pears, peeled, quartered and sliced ½ inch thick
Juice of 1 lemon

Cut up the chicken into serving pieces; sprinkle with the salt, Accent, pepper and flour. Melt the butter in a large skillet and brown the chicken slowly on each side.

Place the chicken in a casserole dish suitable for serving from at the table. Sprinkle the chicken with the nutmeg, cloves and cinnamon. Set aside.

In the butter that remains in the skillet, put the pineapple, juice and all. Add the seedless raisins and wine. Simmer and stir for a few minutes, until you have loosened all the browned material in the skillet. Pour this mixture over the chicken. Cover, and place in a 350° F. oven for 1 hour, or until you can pierce the thickest piece with a fork.

After peeling and slicing the avocados, sprinkle them with the lemon juice and set aside.

After the chicken is tender and done, pour the lemon juice from the avocados over it and mix in slightly. Place the slices of avocado over the top. Bake for 8 minutes longer. Serve piping hot. Serves 4 to 6.

FAR EASTERN CHICKEN

1 3- to 4-pound fryer-broiler, cut into portion-sized pieces
½ cup flour
½ teaspoon salt
¼ teaspoon pepper
½ cup olive oil
1 cup onion, coarsely chopped
1 clove garlic, sliced paper thin
2 cups fresh diced tomatoes
½ cup chopped green pepper
½ cup pine nuts
1 cup hot water with 2 tablespoons instant chicken bouillon
    dissolved in it
½ teaspoon curry powder
1 chili pepper (dried, small red pepper)

Wipe the pieces of chicken with paper toweling. Mix the flour, salt and pepper together. Sprinkle this mixture on all sides of the chicken pieces.

Heat the olive oil in a large skillet and brown the chicken on all sides. Remove the chicken from the oil and place in a casserole with a tight-fitting cover.

Mix the onion, garlic, tomatoes, green pepper and pine nuts and pour this over the chicken. Stir the curry powder into the chicken bouillon mixture and then pour over the chicken and vegetables. Place the chili pepper to one side in the casserole so that it can be removed after the dish is cooked. Cover, and put in a 350° F. oven for 1 hour, or until you can pierce the thickest portion of the chicken with a sharp fork. Serve piping hot. Serves 4.

TURKISH CHICKEN IN QUINCE SHELLS

2 chicken breasts, cut in half
6 ripe quince, about 3 to 4 inches in diameter
2 cups cold water
½ teaspoon salt
¼ teaspoon pepper
¼ cup white bread crumbs
⅛ teaspoon cloves
3 tablespoons sugar
⅛ pound butter

Place the chicken breasts, water, salt and pepper in a saucepan with a tight-fitting cover. Bring to a rolling boil and skim off any froth that may gather on top. Turn the heat back to simmer, cover and cook for 30 minutes, or until the thickest parts of the breasts can be pierced with a fork. Remove from the heat; take out the chicken breasts to cool and set aside the broth.

Peel and core the quince; using your coring tool or a sharp teaspoon, hollow out the quince so that a wall about ½ inch thick is left. Discard the portions you hollow out.

Remove the white meat from the ribcage; discard the bones and skin. Chop the white meat until it is very fine. Add 3 tablespoons of the broth, the bread crumbs and cloves and mix until all is of a smooth consistency. Stuff each of the quince with some of the mixture. Place in a baking pan. Pour 1 cup broth around the outside of the quince. Sprinkle them with the sugar and add a pat of butter to the top of each. Place in a 350° F. oven for 2 hours, or until the quince have turned a delicate shade of pink and are tender when pierced with a sharp fork. Serve at once, piping hot. Serves 6.

TURKISH CHICKEN WITH SESAME SEED

1 2- or 3-pound broiler-fryer, cut into portion-sized pieces
¾ cup flour
½ teaspoon salt
¼ teaspoon pepper
2 teaspoons paprika
2 eggs, beaten until lemon yellow
¼ cup water
¾ cup sesame seeds
Vegetable oil for deep frying

Dry the chicken pieces with paper toweling. Put the flour, salt, pepper and paprika in a paper sack and shake to mix well. Place the chicken, a few pieces at a time, in the seasoned flour and shake vigorously so that it is completely covered.

Add the water to the eggs and mix well. Add the sesame seeds to the remaining flour in the sack and shake well so that the seeds and flour are thoroughly mixed. Dip each piece of chicken in the egg mixture and then in the flour mixture. Again, shake vigorously so that the chicken pieces are covered thoroughly. Drop the chicken pieces into 350° F. cooking oil and fry until they are golden brown.

After the chicken has browned, place it on a rack in a baking pan and continue to cook in a 350° F. oven for 35 minutes, or until the thickest portions can be pierced with a fork. Serve at once, piping hot. Serves 4.

GUATEMALA CHICKEN

1 3-pound frying chicken, cut up into portion-sized pieces
4 tablespoons bacon fat
3 cloves garlic, sliced 1/16 inch thick
3 medium-sized peeled tomatoes, cut into eighths
3 medium-sized fresh pimientos, sliced in 1/4-inch strips
1 tablespoon capers
1 tablespoon caper juice
1/2 cup pimiento-stuffed olives cut in halves
1/2 teaspoon salt
1/4 teaspoon pepper
1/2 cup tomato juice
3 cups hot fluffy cooked rice

In a large skillet, melt the bacon fat and then add the garlic and chicken. Sauté the chicken until it is browned on all sides.

Add the tomatoes, pimientos, capers, caper juice, olives, salt, pepper and tomato juice, and bring to a boil. Cover, and reduce heat to simmer. Cook for 1 hour, or until the thickest portions of the chicken can be easily pierced with a fork.

Place the hot rice around the edge of a deep platter, then arrange the chicken and its sauce in the middle. Serve piping hot. Serves 4.

Chapter VIII

CHICKEN IN A HURRY

EVERY GOOD COOK gets pushed into the frenzy corner at one time or another; she's called upon to provide a feast on very short notice.

It's no pleasure to be rushed. However, it *is* nice to be able to face the dilemma with a confident gleam in your eye and a collection of recipes from which you can make a banquet type meal or a festive main dish in nothing flat. Chicken, because of its tender nature and its wonderful delicate flavor, is one of the few meats that taste good even when prepared in a rush. This chapter contains some of these appetizing dishes that can be whipped up in a hurry.

One of the greatest conveniences to the gal in a rush is frozen chicken parts or frozen broiler-fryer halves. Thawing chicken can be done in minutes if you leave it in its plastic wrapping and just put it under running tap water; if the rush is of the super-desperate variety, you can run the water directly on the raw chicken pieces. There will be a slight loss of good chicken flavor if you do this, but it will probably never be missed when the family enjoys what you have whipped up at top speed.

If you can dent the thawing chicken or flex it with a little effort, you are ready to start cooking it. Even if it isn't thoroughly thawed, you can start the recipe and let the remainder of the thawing take place during the cooking.

If you have the kind of family that likes to surprise you with unexpected guests or complains of being hungry at odd hours, turn to frozen chicken; it can and will save the day. Be a smart chick and learn how to cook "the quick chick" way.

QUICK CHICKEN CASSEROLE

3 chicken breasts, cut in half
½ teaspoon salt
¼ teaspoon pepper
½ teaspoon Accent
¾ cup self-rising pancake mix
½ cup peanut oil
1 cup instant rice
1 10-ounce can cream of chicken soup
¾ cup half and half cream

Wipe the chicken breasts with paper toweling. Sprinkle each half with a portion of the salt, pepper and Accent. Place the pancake mix in a paper sack, then coat each piece of chicken with the mix by shaking up and down vigorously. Heat the oil in a suitable skillet; brown each piece of chicken on both sides.

Cook the rice according to the directions on the package. Stir the cream of chicken soup and the half and half cream into the cooked rice. Put the soup and rice mixture into a buttered casserole, then put the pieces of chicken breast over the top. Place in a 350° F. oven for 35 minutes. Serve piping hot. Serves 6.

CHICKEN LIVERS SMOTHERED IN ONIONS

1 pound chicken livers
½ teaspoon salt
¼ teaspoon pepper
¼ cup chicken fat, margarine or butter
2 cups sweet onions, sliced about ⅛-inch thick
1 cup mushroom stems and pieces

Cut up the chicken livers into bite-sized pieces. Sprinkle them with salt and pepper and allow them to stand a few minutes to absorb the seasonings. Melt the chicken fat in a large skillet with a tight-fitting cover. Add the chicken livers and sauté them until they begin to brown and can be cut with a fork.

Add the onions and mushrooms and cover the skillet. Cook over low heat for 10 minutes. Remove the cover and turn up the heat slightly. Turn the livers and onions over with a spatula and sauté for 5 minutes longer, or until the onions turn a golden brown. Serve at once. Serves 4.

QUICK CHICKEN AND PARSLEY DUMPLINGS

1 3-pound broiler, cut up into portion-sized pieces
¾ cup all-purpose flour
½ teaspoon salt
¼ teaspoon pepper
¼ teaspoon garlic salt
1 teaspoon paprika
3 tablespoons peanut oil
1 10-ounce can cream of mushroom soup
1½ cups dairy sour cream

Parsley Dumplings:

1½ cups sifted all-purpose flour
3 teaspoons baking powder
½ teaspoon salt
⅓ cup milk
2 eggs, beaten until lemon yellow
¼ cup fresh parsley, chopped fine, or 2 tablespoons dehydrated parsley
¼ teaspoon nutmeg

Sift the flour, salt, pepper, garlic salt and paprika together until all is blended. Lay out the pieces of chicken on a sheet of waxed paper and sprinkle them on all sides with the flour mixture. Let them stand for a few minutes, then sprinkle again until you have used up all the seasoned flour. Place the oil in a skillet and brown each piece of chicken on all sides. Pour off any excess oil. Add the mushroom soup and sour cream. Stir well, loosening any of the crisp browned morsels that may have stuck to the bottom of the skillet. Cover, and turn heat down to simmer for 30 minutes, or until the chicken is tender.

Sift the flour, baking powder and salt together at least three times. Mix the milk with the eggs, parsley and nutmeg. Pour the milk-egg mixture into your sifted ingredients. Mix with a fork until the flour is completely moistened. The mixture need not be smooth; it may have lumps in it. Uncover the simmering chicken and drop the dumpling mixture by spoonsful over the surface. Cover again, and cook for 15 minutes without lifting cover. Break dumplings apart with a fork if they have joined each other during the cooking. Serve at once, piping hot. Serves 6.

Variations:

Omit the dumplings and substitute 4 cups fluffy cooked rice.

Omit the dumplings and substitute baking powder biscuits, split in halves and covered with the chicken and gravy.

Omit the dumplings and substitute 1 8-ounce package of broad egg noodles, cooked separately until they are tender, according to the directions on the package. Place the noodles around the outside edge of a platter and pour the chicken and gravy in the middle.

QUICK CHICKEN IN WINE

1 2- or 3-pound broiler, cut up into portion-sized pieces
½ teaspoon salt
¼ teaspoon pepper
1 cup coarsely chopped onion
½ cup olive oil
¼ cup chopped parsley or 2 tablespoons dehydrated parsley flakes
½ cup wine vinegar
1 cup Chablis wine

Place the chicken in a large baking dish with a tight-fitting cover. Sprinkle with salt and pepper and distribute the onions over and around the chicken. Drizzle the olive oil over all. Sprinkle with parsley. Cover and place in a 350° F. oven for 35 minutes, or until the thickest portions of the chicken can be easily pierced with a fork.

Add the vinegar and wine, cover again and return to the 350° F. oven for an additional 20 minutes. Uncover, and continue to bake for 10 minutes more, or until the top of the chicken turns a delicate brown and the liquid is reduced by half. Serve at once, piping hot. Serves 4.

Variations:

Use ½ cup sweet vermouth and ½ cup dry sherry instead of Chablis.

Use 1 cup Rhine wine instead of the Chablis.

Use chicken legs and thighs instead of a whole chicken.

Use only chicken breasts instead of a whole chicken.

CREAMED CHICKEN SUPREME

The usual kind of creamed chicken always leaves me cold; it seems that the cream sauce overwhelms the chicken or the chicken overwhelms the cream sauce, and the result is a bland-tasting, anonymous concoction. Here is a recipe that takes creamed chicken out of the so-so class and puts it in a new niche. This should be made just minutes before serving. Do not let it stand over hot water for a long time or you will lose the zest of the dish.

4 cups cooked chicken meat, cut into ½-inch cubes
¼ pound butter
4 tablespoons all-purpose flour
2 cups milk
1 tablespoon green pepper, chopped fine
1 tablespoon canned pimiento, chopped fine
1 tablespoon scallions (white part only), chopped fine
1 tablespoon Worcestershire sauce
Dash of cayenne pepper
½ teaspoon salt
2 egg yolks, beaten until lemon yellow
1 cup half and half cream
1½ cups mushroom stems and pieces

Melt the butter in the top portion of a double boiler. Stir in the flour and cook for a few seconds until bubbly. Slowly stir in the milk. Stir until all is well blended. Place the boiler top over boiling water and cook until the sauce is thickened. Stir in the green pepper, pimiento, scallions, Worcestershire sauce, cayenne and salt. Stir for a few seconds to blend.

Stir a few spoonsful of the hot sauce into the eggs, then add the eggs to the sauce. Stir well for a few seconds. Stir in the cream and cook for a few seconds until warmed through. Add the mushrooms and chicken. Stir all very well and cook for a few seconds, or until the chicken and mushrooms are warmed through. Serve immediately. Serves 6.

Variations:

Serve over toast or in toast baskets that you make by putting soft white buttered enriched bread in buttered muffin tins and placing in a 400° F. oven for 5 minutes, or until golden brown.
Serve over chow mein noodles.

Serve in potato baskets (these can be purchased in the bakery section of your supermarket).
Serve over a mound of shoestring potatoes.
Serve over hot cooked broad egg noodles.
Serve over hot cooked fluffy rice.

QUICK CHICKEN 'N DUMPLINGS

1 2½- to 3-pound frying chicken, cut into portion-sized pieces
½ cup chopped onion (reserve 1 tablespoon for the dumplings)
2 thin slices lemon
1 small bay leaf
1 teaspoon salt
¼ teaspoon pepper
2½ cups warm tap water

Dumplings:

1 cup sifted flour
1 teaspoon baking powder
½ teaspoon salt
1 tablespoon chopped onion (reserved from above)
⅛ teaspoon ground nutmeg
2 egg yolks, beaten until lemon yellow
½ cup half and half coffee cream

In a kettle with a tight-fitting cover, place the chicken, onion, lemon, bay leaf, salt, pepper and warm water. Bring to a rolling boil and skim away any froth that gathers. Cover tightly and simmer for 30 minutes, or until the chicken breast can be pierced with a fork. Turn pieces of chicken over once or twice during this cooking period.

Mix well the flour, baking powder, salt, chopped onion and nutmeg. Alternately add the beaten eggs and cream to the flour mixture, stirring after each addition. Mix until all is smoothly blended. Drop teaspoonsful of this mixture on top of the bubbling chicken mixture. Close cover tightly again and cook at simmer for another 15 minutes without opening cover. When ready to serve, break dumplings apart with a fork, arrange on a platter with the chicken, and pour the remaining gravy over all.

CHICKEN CROQUETTES

3 cups cooked chicken, ground or chopped very fine, both light and dark meat
¼ cup melted butter
¼ cup onion, chopped fine
¼ cup all-purpose flour
½ cup warm water with 2 tablespoons of instant chicken bouillon dissolved in it
½ cup milk
¼ teaspoon pepper
¼ teaspoon celery salt
¼ teaspoon thyme
2 tablespoons parsley, chopped fine
1 egg, beaten until lemon yellow
1 tablespoon lemon juice
¼ teaspoon grated lemon rind
¾ cup toasted pecans, chopped fine

Breading mixture:

2 eggs, beaten until lemon yellow, plus 2 tablespoons cold water
2 cups fine cracker crumbs

Put the melted butter in a saucepan; add the onion and cook over low heat for 5 minutes. Stir in the flour and mix until all is smoothly blended. Add the warm water with bouillon and milk. Cook over low heat, stirring constantly until the mixture has become thoroughly blended and thick. Remove from the heat and add the pepper, celery salt, thyme and parsley. Stir a few spoonsful of the mixture into the beaten egg, then add the egg to the mixture. Add the lemon juice and rind and mix all very well.

Add the thick sauce and the pecans to the chicken and mix all thoroughly. Press the mixture into a lightly buttered round cake pan. If you happen to have one of those pans with the metal cake remover that travels over the bottom and up the side, excellent, for this will greatly aid in the removal of the croquettes after they are chilled. Place the cake pan of croquette mixture in the coldest part of the refrigerator for at least three hours, or until chilled through and firm.

When cold and firm, divide the mixture into 6 equal pie-shaped wedges. Remove each wedge, dip into the egg and water mixture and then into the crumbs. Press the crumbs into the surface and sides so that you do not lose too many in the frying process.

Fry in deep fat at 350° F. until the croquettes are a delicate golden brown. Serve at once, piping hot. Serves 6.

Variations:

Substitute toasted almonds, chopped fine, for the pecans.
Substitute toasted Virginia style peanuts, chopped fine, for the pecans.
Serve with creamed peas poured over each croquette.
Use a 10-ounce can of cream of mushroom soup, thoroughly heated but not diluted, as gravy over the croquettes.

Note: Chicken croquettes freeze beautifully. Place them in individual plastic bags after they have been breaded and then freeze immediately. When you need a nourishing meal in a hurry, just drop them as they come from the freezer in 300° F. hot vegetable oil and fry them slowly.

QUICK CHICKEN AND VEGETABLE CASSEROLE

2 cups white meat, cooked and diced
3 cups water
1 10-ounce package frozen peas and carrots
1 10-ounce package frozen French style green beans
1 cup finely shredded outside green leaves of iceberg lettuce
1 teaspoon granulated sugar
2 eggs, beaten until lemon yellow
1 cup milk
1 teaspoon salt
¼ teaspoon pepper
1 4-ounce can mushroom stems and pieces

Bring the three cups of water to a rolling boil; add the peas and carrots and the beans and then bring to a boil again. Remove from the heat and stir in the lettuce and sugar. Set aside for a few minutes. Do not cover.

Meanwhile, mix the eggs, milk, salt and pepper.

Drain the peas and carrots, beans and lettuce. Add the chicken and the mushrooms. Stir all with a light hand. Place in a buttered casserole dish. Pour the milk and egg mixture over all. Bake in a 350° F. oven for 35 minutes, or until the milk mixture has thickened. Serve at once, piping hot. Serves 4.

CHICKEN GIZZARDS WITH HERB RICE

If you have a gizzard or giblet fan in your clan, try this recipe for rave notices.

1 pound chicken gizzards
2 cups cold water
½ teaspoon salt
¼ teaspoon pepper
½ cup chopped onion
6 tablespoons margarine
2 cups instant rice as it comes from the package
½ cup chopped celery
2 tablespoons instant chicken bouillon
¼ cup chopped parsley
¼ teaspoon thyme
¼ teaspoon marjoram
¼ teaspoon savory

Wash the chicken gizzards under cold running water. Place them in a saucepan with the water, salt, pepper and onion. Bring to a rolling boil, then skim off any froth that may gather. Cover, reduce heat, and cook at simmer for 30 minutes, or until tender enough to pierce with a fork. Remove the gizzards from the broth and set them aside.

Measure the broth; you should have 2 cups or a little more. Add enough water to make 4 cups. Melt 3 tablespoons of margarine in a saucepan large enough to hold 4 cups of cooked rice. Put the instant rice in the margarine over low heat. Sauté until the rice begins to brown. Add the celery and the broth and turn up heat so that the rice reaches a rolling boil. Stir in the chicken bouillon and the parsley. Add the thyme, marjoram and savory. Stir the mixture for a second or so to mix well; cover and lower heat to simmer. Cook for 15 minutes without taking off the cover.

Meanwhile, place the remaining 3 tablespoons of margarine in a skillet over low heat. Cut up the chicken gizzards into bite-sized pieces and place in the margarine. Sauté until they begin to get brown. Add ¼ cup water, cover and simmer for 10 minutes.

Put the rice in the middle of a deep platter. Place the chicken gizzards around the outside; pour the water and margarine from the gizzards over the rice. Serve at once, piping hot. Serves 4.

Variations:

Substitute assorted chicken giblets for the gizzards.

Substitute chicken livers for the gizzards and diminish the boiling time to 20 minutes, or until they are tender.

Omit the thyme, marjoram and savory if you prefer plain chicken-flavored rice.

Add 1 cup of mushroom stems and pieces to the gizzards as you are sautéing them.

Garnish the top of the rice with strips of pimiento if you want more color.

QUICK CHINESE CHICKEN

2 chicken breasts, cut in half
1 cup cold water
½ teaspoon salt
¼ teaspoon pepper
2 tablespoons butter
¼ cup chopped onion
1 10-ounce can cream of mushroom soup
2 cups celery, sliced diagonally ⅛ inch thick
½ cup roasted salted almonds, coarsely chopped
1 cup chow mein noodles
1 8-ounce can mandarin oranges, drained
2 tablespoons soy sauce

In a skillet with a tight-fitting cover, put the chicken breasts, skin side down, the water, salt and pepper, and bring to a rolling boil. Skim off any froth and continue to cook over moderate heat, covered tightly, for 35 minutes. Remove breasts to cool; strain and measure the broth left in the pan.

After the chicken is cool enough to handle, remove the skin and bones and discard. Cut up the white meat into bite-sized pieces.

Melt the butter in a skillet and add the onion; cook over moderate heat until the onion is transparent and glazed. Add the soup, 1 cup of the reserved chicken broth, celery, almonds and chicken. Cook over moderate heat for 10 minutes. Then add half of the chow mein noodles, the orange segments and the soy sauce. Cook for 5 minutes longer. Serve in a deep platter with a sprinkle of the remainder of the chow mein noodles. Serves 4.

QUICKIE CHICKEN AND RICE

1 2- or 3-pound broiler, cut up into portion-sized pieces
½ teaspoon salt
¼ teaspoon pepper
½ teaspoon Accent
1 teaspoon paprika
1 cup packaged instant rice
1 package onion soup mix
1 10-ounce can cream of chicken soup
2 cups warm water

Wipe the chicken pieces with paper toweling. Mix the salt, pepper, Accent and paprika together and sprinkle the pieces of chicken well. Set them aside.

Mix together the rice, soup mix, soup and water. Let stand for 5 minutes, then pour into a 9″ x 13″ baking pan. Put the pieces of seasoned chicken on top of the mixture. Place, uncovered, in a 350° F. oven and bake for 45 minutes, or until the rice is puffed up and the chicken is tender. Serve at once, piping hot. Serves 4.

Variations:

Substitute 1 10-ounce can of cream of celery soup for the chicken soup.
Substitute 1 10-ounce can of cream of mushroom soup for the chicken soup.
Use 1 10-ounce can of cream of mushroom soup along with the chicken soup, and diminish the warm water by 1 cup.
Add ¼ cup parsley, chopped fine, to the chicken soup and rice mixture.
Add ¼ cup celery, chopped fine, to the chicken soup and rice mixture.
Substitute three chicken breasts, cut in halves, for the whole chicken.
Substitute three chicken legs and thighs for the whole chicken.

SKILLET CHICKEN 'N GRAVY

2 2- to 3-pound fryer-broilers, cut up into portion-sized pieces
1½ cups flour
½ cup white corn meal
1 teaspoon salt
¼ teaspoon pepper
1 teaspoon Accent
½ cup vegetable oil
¼ pound butter
3½ cups warm water

Wipe the pieces of chicken with paper toweling. Mix the flour, corn meal, salt, pepper and Accent in a paper sack. Place several pieces of chicken in the sack at a time and shake up and down until they are thoroughly coated with the flour mixture.

Place the vegetable oil in a large skillet with a tight-fitting cover. Brown the chicken on all sides. Remove from the skillet and pour off any excess oil.

Put the butter and warm water in the skillet and heat until the butter is melted and just beginning to boil. Place the browned chicken in this mixture; bring to a slow simmer, cover tightly, and cook for 35 minutes, or until the chicken is tender and the gravy is thickened. Serve at once, piping hot. Serves 6.

Variations:

Add 1 10-ounce package of mushrooms frozen in butter sauce 5 minutes before serving.

Add 1 #2 can Chinese style chow mein vegetables, drained, 5 minutes before serving.

Top with simple dumplings as soon as the chicken is tender, cover again and cook 15 minutes longer, or until the dumplings are puffy and done). Use the dumpling recipe given with Quick Chicken and Dumplings, page 97.

CHICKEN AND CHIP CASSEROLE

3 cups cooked cubed chicken, light and dark meat
1 cup instant rice as it comes from the package
1 10-ounce can cream of chicken soup
¾ cup milk
4 tablespoons butter
½ cup celery, chopped fine
¼ cup onion, chopped fine
1 10-ounce package mushrooms frozen in butter sauce
3 cups potato chips, crushed fine

Mix the rice, chicken soup and milk. Set aside while you prepare the rest.

Melt the butter in a saucepan and add the celery and onion; cook over low heat until the onion is glazed and transparent. Remove from the heat and stir in the frozen mushrooms. Then stir in the chicken. Add this to the rice and chicken soup and mix all well.

Put 1½ cups of the crushed potato chips in the bottom of a buttered casserole. Mound them up somewhat along the sides. Carefully pour in the chicken, rice and vegetable mixture. Top with the remainder of the potato chips. Bake in a 325° F. oven for 35 minutes, or until the chips have turned a rich brown. Serve at once, piping hot. Serves 6.

Variations:

Substitute 1 10-ounce package of frozen peas or 1 #2 can of peas, drained, for the mushrooms.
Substitute 1 10-ounce can of cream of mushroom soup for the chicken soup.
Substitute 2 cups of cooked rice for the instant, if you happen to have it on hand. Diminish the milk to ½ cup.

CHICKEN 'N PEAS

2 cups diced cooked chicken, both light and dark meat
2 cups small white onions
5 tablespoons butter
5 tablespoons flour
½ teaspoon salt
¼ teaspoon pepper
1 tablespoon Worcestershire sauce
2½ cups milk
1 10-ounce package frozen peas, thawed to room temperature
1 10-ounce package mushrooms frozen in butter sauce

Peel the onions and cook them in 1 cup water in a tightly covered saucepan until they are tender but not broken apart. Drain and set aside.

Melt the butter in a saucepan, stir in the flour and cook over low heat until it begins to bubble. Add the salt, pepper, Worcestershire sauce and milk. Cook, stirring constantly, over low heat until the sauce is thick and smooth. Add the diced chicken and onions to the sauce; then add the peas and mushrooms. Continue to cook over low heat until all is heated through. Serve in potato baskets. Serves 4.

Variations:

Use two 9-ounce cans of little onions, drained, if you are in a rush. Just warm them through with the rest of the ingredients.
Add ¼ cup of diced pimiento just before serving if you want more color.
Serve over chow mein noodles if you do not have potato baskets.
Top each serving with a sprinkle of chopped toasted pecans for a unique flavor addition.

QUICK CHICKEN SOUFFLÉ

3 cups cooked chicken meat, diced into ½-inch pieces
½ teaspoon salt
¼ teaspoon pepper
1 10-ounce can golden cream of mushroom soup
1 10-ounce can cream of chicken soup
1 4-ounce can mushroom buttons, drained
4 tablespoons butter
4 tablespoons flour
1 cup milk
¼ teaspoon salt
⅛ teaspoon pepper
5 eggs, separated

In a mixing bowl, combine the chicken, salt, pepper, mushroom soup, chicken soup and mushrooms. Stir well, and set aside so the flavors can unite.

In the top of the double boiler melt the butter; stir in the flour and cook over low heat until the flour begins to bubble. Add the milk and stir well until blended. Place the double boiler top over boiling water and continue to cook, stirring constantly, until the sauce is thick. Add the salt and pepper. Beat the egg yolks until they are lemon colored. Stir a few spoonsful of the hot sauce into the eggs, then add the eggs to the sauce. Stir well. Remove from the heat and allow to cool for a few seconds.

Beat the egg whites until they stand in peaks. Fold the sauce into the egg whites; be sure to use a gentle folding action so you do not lose the air in the eggs.

Pour the soup and chicken mixture into a buttered baking dish. Top this with the sauce and egg whites. Place in a pan of warm water in a 300° F. oven for 15 minutes. Then increase the heat to 325° F. and bake for 25 minutes longer, or until a table knife inserted in the top layer comes out clean. Serve piping hot. Serves 6.

When serving, be careful to dip down to the bottom of the baking dish so that each portion contains both the soufflé topping and a portion of the chicken mixture. Invert each serving so that the chicken mixture coats the soufflé portion.

Variations:

Double the cream sauce portion of the recipe and omit the soups.

Fold in the egg whites, chicken and mushrooms all at once and then bake.

Add 1 cup of grated Swiss cheese to the soufflé topping for a different flavor.

Add 1 cup of grated American cheese to the soufflé topping.

Add ½ cup of grated Parmesan cheese to the soufflé topping.

Line the bottom of the baking dish with 1 cup of crushed potato chips before putting in the chicken mixture.

Add 2 tablespoons of canned pimiento, diced fine, to the chicken mixture.

Add ½ cup of chopped, toasted almonds to the chicken mixture

Add ½ cup of chopped, toasted pecans to the chicken mixture.

Use 2 cans of mushroom soup and omit the chicken soup.

CHICKEN AND BROCCOLI BAKE

3 cups diced cooked chicken, both light and dark meat
2 cups dairy sour cream
1 package onion soup mix
2 packages frozen broccoli, cooked according to the directions on the package
1 cup whipping cream (No imitation whips, please!)
2 tablespoons grated Parmesan cheese
¼ teaspoon paprika

Mix the sour cream and the onion soup until smooth and completely blended. Put half the broccoli in the bottom of a buttered casserole. Dot this with spoonsful of the sour cream mixture. Sprinkle half of the cooked chicken over the broccoli and cream; dot the chicken with spoonsful of the sour cream and then add another layer of broccoli; again dot with some of the sour cream.

Whip the whipping cream until it stands in peaks. Carefully fold in the remainder of the sour cream-onion soup mixture. Spread this over the top of the casserole. Sprinkle with cheese. Dust the paprika over the top. Place in a 325° F. oven for 30 minutes, or until the top is golden brown and bubbly. Serve piping hot. Serves 6.

CHICKEN PATTIES AND CELERY ROOT

3 cups cooked chicken, both light and dark meat
4 slices enriched white bread
½ cup hot water with 1 tablespoon instant chicken bouillon
    dissolved in it
2 4-inch diameter celery roots, soaked overnight
½ cup chopped celery
3 eggs, beaten until lemon yellow
¼ teaspoon freshly grated nutmeg
¼ cup peanut oil

Chop the chicken until it is very fine or put it through a
food chopper. Soak the bread slices in the hot water with the
chicken bouillon. Squeeze out any excess water and add to the
chicken along with the celery, eggs and nutmeg. Mix all very
well. Form into 3-inch diameter patties about ¾ inch thick.
Using half the oil, brown each patty on both sides. Remove
the patties from the oil and set aside while you prepare the
celery root.

Peel the celery root and cut it (only the center portion)
into ¼-inch slices. Save the tapered ends for soup. Put the
slices in the same skillet in which you browned the patties.
Add more oil and sauté until the slices begin to get golden
brown on both sides. Pour off any excess oil.

Place a browned patty on top of each piece of celery root.
Add enough water just to come up to the top of the slice of
celery root, cover and cook over low heat for 45 minutes. Add
more water from time to time if necessary. Serve piping hot.
Serves 6.

PILAFF WITH CHICKEN LIVERS

½ pound chicken livers
1 #3 (46-fluid-ounce) can chicken broth
Peanut oil
1 cup raw shredded carrots
1 cup onions, sliced thin
½ cup loosely packed chopped parsley
½ teaspoon turmeric
½ teaspoon salt
¼ teaspoon pepper
2 tablespoons instant chicken bouillon
1½ cups long grain rice
2 cups fresh tomato, peeled and cut into 1-inch cubes
1 clove garlic, minced fine

Skim off any fat that has gathered on top of the can of chicken broth. Measure the fat, and bring it up to ½ cup by adding peanut oil. Put this in a skillet over low heat. Set the broth aside until later.

Put the chicken livers in the heated fat and oil and sauté until they are tender; then remove them from the fat and set aside to cool. Add the carrots, onion and parsley to the remaining fat and sauté for a few minutes, until the carrots begin to get tender.

Dice the chicken livers into ¼-inch cubes and add to the vegetables. Stir in the turmeric, salt and pepper. Add the broth you have set aside; add the chicken bouillon and stir over low heat until it is dissolved. Add the rice, cover, and cook over moderate heat for 20 minutes, or until it is light and doubled in size. Stir in the tomato and garlic. Do not cover; cook for an additional 15 minutes. Serve at once, piping hot. Serves 4.

CHICKEN-BANANA-ORANGE MEDLEY

2 cups cooked chicken white meat, cut into ½-inch cubes
4 bananas, cut lengthwise
3 seedless oranges, peeled and sliced into ¼-inch slices
½ teaspoon Accent
½ teaspoon salt
½ cup butter
2 tablespoons lemon juice
¼ cup honey

Place the bananas in a baking dish side by side. Distribute the chicken cubes over and around them. Place the sliced oranges over the bananas. Sprinkle with the Accent and salt. Dot all over with pieces of butter. Mix the lemon juice and honey and pour over all. Place in 275° F. oven for 35 minutes. Serve at once. Serves 4.

This is excellent, easy-to-make summer dish that will arouse jaded summer appetites. Serve with hot buttermilk biscuits or baking powder biscuits and a green salad for a meal that will please all.

CHEESE PINWHEELS AND CHICKEN

3 cups cooked diced chicken, both light and dark meat
2 tablespoons butter
¾ cup celery, cut diagonally ⅛ inch thick
¼ cup onion, diced in ¼-inch cubes
2 tablespoons flour
1 cup boiling water with 2 tablespoons instant chicken bouillon dissolved in it
2 cups prepared biscuit mix
1 cup pimiento American cheeese, grated or broken into small pieces

Put the butter in a saucepan; add the celery and onion and cook over low heat until the onion is transparent and glazed and the celery is tender. Sprinkle the flour into the celery and onion mixture, stirring until all is well mixed. Add the boiling water and bouillon and cook over low heat until thickened, stirring constantly. Add the chicken; stir well, then remove from heat.

Prepare the biscuit dough for biscuits according to package directions. Place the soft dough on a floured board and roll and pat until it is oblong in shape and about ½ inch thick. Sprinkle the cheese over the top of the dough. Starting at one end of the dough, roll up, jelly roll fashion; seal the edge with a few drops of water. Using a sharp knife dipped in water, slice through the roll, making ½-inch slices.

Place the chicken mixture in a buttered baking dish, then put the pinwheel rolls over the top. Bake in a 375° F. oven for 25 minutes, or until the pinwheels are puffy and delicate brown. Serve piping hot. Serves 6.

Chapter IX

CHICKEN SALADS

CHICKEN SALAD IS a wonderful way to satisfy hungry people. These salads offer a protein punch with a zesty flavor no one will pass up.

Stewing chicken, cooked until tender, then divorced of its bones and skin, makes the best salads. It is wise to cook the chicken in as little water as possible in order to retain all its food value. If you own a pressure cooker, pressure cooking is ideal.

Some cooks like to boil a chicken to get soup out of it first and then use the remainder of the chicken for salads. I always feel you are selling your family short on nourishment if you do this. The resulting soup is never really hearty, due to the lack of chicken pieces in it, and the salad turns out to be a bland, tasteless affair because all its good flavor stayed in the soup. Your sense of economy may compel you to make soup first and then use the cold chicken for salad. But do try it the extravagant way; you will notice a big difference. Just cook that chicken with salad alone in mind. Freeze in an ice cube tray the small amount of broth you will have left over, then use it to add zip and flavor to your next weak batch of gravy. You can use just two or three cubes at a time, as you need them, and keep the remainder frozen.

CHICKEN, PEAS AND CHEESE

2 cups cooked chicken, diced into ½-inch pieces
1 cup American cheese, diced into ¼-inch pieces
1 10-ounce package frozen baby peas, thawed to room temperature
½ cup mayonnaise
Lettuce leaves

Mix together all ingredients but the lettuce. Serve on lettuce leaves. Serves 4.

CHICKEN SALAD

2 cups diced chicken white meat
1 cup celery, diced into ¼-inch pieces
2 hard-boiled eggs, coarsely chopped
1 tablespoon onion, chopped fine
1 tablespoon India relish
¼ cup mayonnaise
½ teaspoon salt
¼ teaspoon white pepper
4 medium-sized tomatoes
1 small head iceberg lettuce, shredded fine

Combine the chicken, celery, eggs, onion, relish, mayonnaise, salt and pepper. Toss together with a light hand.

Cut the tops off the tomatoes; scoop out a portion of the pulp and discard. Fill each tomato with a portion of the chicken salad and put each tomato on a portion of the shredded lettuce. Chill for ½ hour in the refrigerator before serving.

MIAMI CHICKEN SALAD

3 cups of cooked diced chicken
2 cups fresh grapefruit sections
1½ cups of diagonally cut celery, ⅛ inch thick
¼ teaspoon grated lime peel
2 tablespoons lime juice
½ cup mayonnaise
½ teaspoon salt
¼ teaspoon pepper
2 oranges, peeled and sliced ¼ inch thick
Endive

Mix together the grapefruit, chicken and celery. Add the lime peel and lime juice to the mayonnaise. Add the salt and pepper. Beat with a rotary beater until mixed and fluffy. Fold this into the chicken mixture. Line a salad bowl with snipped endive. Place the chicken salad in the center; arrange the orange slices around the outside edge over the endive. Chill in the refrigerator for 1 hour. Serves 6.

CHICKEN-OLIVE SALAD

2 cups cooked diced chicken white meat
1 cup diced celery, cut in ¼-inch cubes
½ cup pimiento olives, sliced
½ cup ripe olives, sliced
2 tablespoons unflavored gelatin
¼ cup cold water
1 cup boiling water
1 teaspoon prepared mustard
½ teaspoon Accent
½ teaspoon salt
2 tablespoons cider vinegar
2 tablespoons granulated sugar
2 tablespoons peanut oil
2 tablespoons chili sauce
2 eggs, beaten until lemon yellow

Mix the chicken, celery and olives well. Place all the ingredients in a slightly oiled mold.

Soften the gelatin in the cold water for 8 minutes, then stir it into the boiling water. Stir until all is dissolved. Add the mustard, Accent, salt, vinegar, sugar, peanut oil, chili sauce and eggs. Stir well so that all of the ingredients are mixed and blended. Pour this mixture over the chicken and vegetables in the mold. Place in the refrigerator for at least 3 hours, or until firm.

Unmold on a bed of shredded lettuce. Serves 6.

CHICKEN SALAD WITH FRUIT

3 cups cooked diced chicken, cut in ½-inch cubes
3 bananas, diced into ½-inch cubes
3 tablespoons lemon juice
1 cup shredded pineapple, drained
2 cups celery, cut into ½-inch cubes
1 teaspoon salt
¾ cup mayonnaise
¼ cup sour cream

Place the diced bananas in a mixing bowl; sprinkle the lemon juice over them. Add the chicken, pineapple and celery. Sprinkle the salt over all. Mix the mayonnaise and sour cream thoroughly. Fold the mayonnaise into the other ingredients. Serve on beds of shredded lettuce or on a bed of endive. Serves 6.

113

CRANBERRY AND CHICKEN SALAD

3 cups cooked chicken white meat diced into ½-inch cubes
1 package strawberry-flavored gelatin
1 cup boiling water
1 #2 can jellied cranberry sauce
1 cup celery, diagonally sliced ⅛ inch thick
¼ cup diced canned pimiento, ¼-inch cubes
¼ teaspoon grated lemon rind
1 tablespoon lemon juice
¾ cup mayonnaise
Lettuce leaves

Dissolve the gelatin in the water. Put the cranberry sauce in the top of the double broiler over slowly boiling water; stir until dissolved and softened. Add the gelatin to the cranberry sauce; mix very well. Pour into a ring mold and place in the refrigerator until firm.

Mix the chicken, celery and pimiento together. Add the lemon rind and lemon juice to the mayonnaise and mix well. Add to the chicken mixture, folding in with a light hand.

Unmold the strawberry-cranberry ring on a bed of lettuce; place the chicken salad in the middle. Serves 6.

CHICKEN AND WALNUT SALAD

3 cups cooked diced chicken, both light and dark meat
2 cups celery, cut diagonally ⅛ inch thick
1½ cups walnut meats, broken into pieces
4 tablespoons Indian pickle relish
¼ cup onion, chopped fine
3 hard-boiled eggs, coarsely chopped
1 cup mayonnaise
½ cup sour cream
3 tablespoons lemon juice

Mix together the chicken, celery, walnuts, pickle relish, onion, eggs and mayonnaise. Mix the sour cream and lemon juice together and fold into the chicken mixture. Place in the refrigerator for 1 hour. Serve on shredded lettuce. Serves 6.

FREEZER TRAY CHICKEN SALAD

Here is an excellent salad to serve when the temperatures soar into the nineties and appetites seem to hit a new low.

2 cups cooked chicken meat, both light and dark, diced in ¼-inch cubes
1 cup crushed pineapple, drained very dry
1 cup coarsely chopped toasted pecans
½ cup marshmallows, snipped into ¼-inch cubes
½ cup canned pimiento, chopped fine
¾ cup mayonnaise
½ teaspoon salt
¼ teaspoon pepper
1 cup whipping cream, whipped until it stands in peaks (no substitutes, please)
2 cups lettuce, shredded

Mix together the first 8 ingredients until well blended. Fold in the whipped cream, taking care not to lose the air and fluffiness. Pour into a large, lightly oiled freezer tray or into a lightly oiled loaf pan and place in the freezing compartment of the refrigerator for 2 hours, or until the center is firm to the touch.

Arrange the shredded lettuce on a platter and unmold the salad loaf in the center. Using a very sharp knife, cut the loaf into six equal portions. Serve each portion on a bed of the shredded lettuce. Serves 6.

DIXIE CHICKEN SALAD

2 cups cooked chicken white meat, diced in ½-inch cubes
2 cups cooked sweet potatoes, diced in ½-inch cubes
2 4-ounce cans mandarin oranges, drained
2 cups diced celery, cut in ½-inch cubes
1 tablespoon lemon juice
¾ cup mayonnaise
Lettuce leaves

Mix the chicken, potatoes, mandarin oranges, celery, lemon juice and mayonnaise well. Place in the refrigerator for 2 hours to chill through.

Serve on lettuce leaves. Serves 6.

HOT CHICKEN SALAD #1

3 cups diced chicken, light and dark meat
1 cup celery, diced in ¼-inch pieces
½ teaspoon salt
¼ teaspoon pepper
¾ cup coarsely chopped walnuts
1 tablespoon grated onion
Juice of ½ lemon
1 cup mayonnaise
1 #2 can chow mein noodles

Mix together the chicken, celery, salt, pepper, walnuts and grated onion. Combine the lemon juice with the mayonnaise and whip until fluffy. Combine this with the chicken mixture; toss all lightly to mix well.

Place the ingredients in a buttered casserole and spread the chow mein noodles over the top. Place in a 350° F. oven for 20 minutes. Serve at once on shredded iceberg lettuce. Serves 4.

HOT CHICKEN SALAD #2

2 cups diced chicken, both light and dark meat
2 10-ounce packages frozen peas
3 cups water
1 cup shredded outside leaves from iceberg lettuce
2 teaspoons granulated sugar
4 tablespoons butter
½ cup slivered almonds
1 4-ounce can mushroom stems and pieces, drained
2 tablespoons lemon juice

Bring the water to a rapid boil. Add the peas and let come to a boil again. Add the lettuce and sugar and remove from heat. Let stand while you prepare the rest.

Put the butter in a skillet, add the almonds and sauté until they begin to turn a golden brown. Add the chicken and mushrooms. Continue to cook for 5 to 8 minutes, or until the chicken is warmed through. Remove from the heat and stir in the lemon juice.

Drain the peas and lettuce; stir in the chicken mixture. Serve at once, while hot, on beds of shredded lettuce.

Variations:

Substitute ½ cup coarsely chopped pecans for the almonds.

Substitute ½ cup shelled pistachio nuts for the almonds, but do not sauté them in the butter. Just heat the chicken and mushrooms and then add the nuts.

Serve on sprigs of water cress instead of the shredded lettuce.

Sprinkle each serving with chow mein noodles if you have to stretch the salad into more portions or if you want a heartier dish.

CHICKEN SALAD SUPREME

3 cups diced cooked chicken, both light and dark meat
1 cup celery, diced in ½-inch pieces
¼ cup scallions, diced fine
½ cup diced green pepper
1 medium-sized avocado pear, diced
1 cup mayonnaise
Dash of cayenne
½ teaspoon salt
¼ teaspoon pepper
Juice of ½ lemon
½ cup dairy sour cream

Mix the chicken, celery, scallions, green pepper, and avocado. Combine the mayonnaise, cayenne, salt, pepper, lemon juice and sour cream. Beat well, until light and fluffy.

Pour the dressing over the chicken mixture and toss lightly so that all is well coated with dressing.

Serve on Boston lettuce or in iceberg lettuce cups. If you want a little color, add strips of pimiento or a sprinkle of paprika over each portion. Serves 4.

CHICKEN SALAD WITH HAZELNUTS

3 cups diced cooked chicken
1½ cups celery, diced in ½-inch pieces
1 teaspoon grated onion
1 cup coarsely chopped roasted hazelnuts
1 cup mayonnaise
½ teaspoon salt
¼ teaspoon pepper

Combine the chicken, celery, onion and the hazelnuts. Add the mayonnaise, salt and pepper. Toss all lightly, making sure the pieces are coated with dressing. Serve on lettuce leaves.

A wonderful companion to this salad is jellied cranberry rounds. If you prefer to make a large platter of salad instead of individual servings, use the jellied cranberry rings as a decorative garnish.

Roasted hazelnuts are obtained from almost any good nut shop. However, if you are able to find only the unroasted type, you can roast them in the oven with a tablespoon or two of butter or oil.

JELLIED CHICKEN SALAD

2 cups cooked chicken, chopped fine
1 cup celery, chopped fine
1 tablespoon minced onion
¼ cup diced canned pimiento, cut in ¼-inch cubes
2 tablespoons unflavored gelatin
½ cup cold water
1 cup boiling water with 2 tablespoons instant chicken bouillon in it
3 tablespoons cider vinegar

Mix the chicken, celery, onion and pimiento together well.

Place the gelatin in the cold water for 5 minutes, or until it is softened. Add the softened gelatin to the boiling water with chicken bouillon dissolved in it. Stir until the gelatin is completely dissolved. Add the cider vinegar. Add to the chicken mixture and mix well. Place in a lightly oiled mold or in a loaf pan. Chill in the refrigerator for at least 4 hours. Unmold on a bed of shredded lettuce. Serves 6.

CHICKEN-ALMOND SALAD BOWL

3 cups cooked chicken, diced in ½-inch pieces
1½ cups celery, chopped fine
½ cup diced avocado pear
2 tablespoons lemon juice
1 cup toasted slivered almonds
¾ cup mayonnaise
¼ teaspoon salt
½ head of lettuce

Mix the chicken and the celery together. Sprinkle the lemon juice over the avocado pear; add to the chicken and celery along with ½ cup of almonds. Fold together carefully and then add the mayonnaise. Again fold with care.

Place the lettuce around the edge of a salad bowl. Arrange the chicken mixture inside the ring of lettuce. Sprinkle the remainder of the slivered almonds over the top. Chill in the refrigerator for 1 hour. Serves 6.

FRENCH BEAN AND CHICKEN SALAD

2 cups cooked chicken, diced into ½-inch cubes
1 #2 can French style green beans, drained
½ cup French dressing
1 drop Tabasco
2 cups shredded lettuce
3 tablespoons olive butter (available in the sandwich spread section of most supermarkets)
1 cup tomato, diced in ½-inch cubes
1 tablespoon minced onion
½ cup celery, chopped fine
¼ cup canned pimiento, diced in ¼-inch cubes

Mix the green beans, chicken, French dressing and Tabasco together. Place in the refrigerator to chill for a half hour.

Stir in the shredded lettuce, olive butter, tomato, onion, celery and pimiento. Toss until all is evenly mixed. Serve at once on lettuce leaves or endive. Serves 6.

SWEET AND SOUR CHICKEN SALAD

2 cups cooked diced chicken, both light and dark meat
10 10-inch-long strips bacon
¾ cup granulated sugar
¾ cup cider vinegar
¼ teaspoon seasoned pepper (found in the spice section of supermarkets)
1 teaspoon celery seed
¼ teaspoon dill seed
2 tablespoons grated onion
½ cup green pepper, cut into ¼-inch cubes
½ cup canned pimientos, cut into ¼-inch cubes
3 cups cooked hot fluffy rice
3 hard-boiled eggs, peeled and sliced

Place the strips of bacon in a skillet over low heat. Sauté until the bacon is golden brown and very crisp, then remove it from the skillet. To the bacon grease that has gathered in the skillet add the sugar, vinegar and seasoned pepper. Stir and cook over low heat until the sugar is all dissolved. Add the celery seed, dill seed, onion, green pepper and pimientos. Continue to cook over low heat and stir in the pieces of chicken.

When all is heated through, spread the hot rice on a deep platter and pour the chicken mixture over it. Crumble the pieces of bacon and sprinkle these over the top. Arrange the egg slices around the edge of the platter. Serve at once, piping hot. Serves 6.

This is a good substitute for potato salad for a patio buffet. It also makes an excellent one-dish meal for very hot days.

Chapter X

CHICKEN ORIENTAL

THERE IS A Chinese restaurant in our city that has the greatest number of dishes containing chicken I have ever seen. My husband is very fond of Oriental cooking; going to this restaurant has forced me to attempt to emulate their cooking, time and time again. I probably have cooked dozens of chickens just trying to imitate their delicious chicken soup alone.

Going to Oriental restaurants has become a family hobby; on every trip we take, we immediately locate the town's Oriental restaurant. We have eaten good food and some that is not worth mentioning. Collecting Oriental recipes is harder than it sounds. Measure ingredients? That's nonsense to most Orientals. The recipes contained in this chapter have been set down in measurements I arrived at via the experimental route. It wasn't easy, because even our cats wouldn't eat some of my mistakes.

The first thing you have to do to be a successful Oriental cook is to print for yourself a big sign with letters four inches tall that reads: DO NOT OVERCOOK ORIENTAL DISHES. The delectable flavors Oriental cooks attain arise from the fact that each ingredient retains its own identity. And most of their foods are usually served with a subtle sauce or gravy.

An Oriental cook can get more flavor out of a chicken than anyone I've ever known. Like the subtle colors and the fine touch in their paintings and art is their use of spices and flavorings in cooking. The light touch is especially important when you are cooking chicken in the Oriental manner.

This chapter contains Chinese, Japanese and many other Oriental chicken dishes. All of the ingredients used are easily obtainable. My personal collection contains many dishes that have unusual Oriental ingredients, but I have purposely omitted these because of the difficulty of obtaining some of these things.

CHICKEN LEGS, ORIENTAL STYLE

6 chicken legs, thigh and all
1 cup flour
¾ cup butter
1 teaspoon salt
¼ teaspoon pepper
1 teaspoon garlic powder
1 #2 can chicken broth
3 tablespoons lemon juice
½ teaspoon grated lemon rind
¼ cup soy sauce
¼ cup candied ginger, chopped fine
3 tablespoons cornstarch dissolved in 1 cup water
¾ cup mushroom stems and pieces

Cut the chicken legs in half at the joint. Place the flour in a sack, and shake the chicken legs in it until they are thoroughly covered with flour. Melt the butter in a large skillet and sauté the chicken until golden brown.

Add the salt, pepper, garlic powder and chicken broth. Reduce the heat, cover, and simmer for 45 minutes, or until the thickest portions of the leg can be pierced with a fork.

Put the chicken in a serving dish and place in a 250° F. oven to keep warm while you make the rest of the sauce. To the broth left in the skillet, add the lemon juice, lemon rind, soy sauce and ginger. Raise the heat to a slow rolling boil, then stir in the cornstarch and water. Stirring constantly, cook until thickened. Add the mushrooms and cook a few seconds longer, until they are warmed through. Pour this mixture over the chicken legs. Serve at once, piping hot. Serves 6. Delicious with hot fluffy rice.

CHICKEN CURRY

2 cups cooked diced chicken, both light and dark meat
3 tart apples, cored and diced in ½-inch pieces
½ cup sweet onion, diced in ½-inch pieces
¼ cup soft butter
1 teaspoon curry
3 tablespoons flour
1 cup milk
1 #2 can chicken broth
½ teaspoon salt
¼ teaspoon pepper
4 cups cooked fluffy rice

Put the apples, onion and butter in a saucepan and sauté over low heat until the onion is transparent and soft. Stir in the curry and flour; add the milk and chicken broth and continue to cook over low heat until slightly thickened. Stir frequently to prevent lumps and sticking.

Add the salt, pepper and chicken and continue to cook 5 minutes longer, or until the chicken is heated through.

Divide the hot rice into four equal portions and top with the curry mixture. Serve piping hot. Serves 4.

Variations:

Use 1 10-ounce can of cream of chicken soup in place of the chicken broth. Add 1 additional cup of milk.
Decrease the curry to ½ teaspoon, for a milder flavored dish.
Serve over boiled noodles instead of rice.

KOREAN STYLE CHICKEN #1

1 3-pound broiler
¼ cup soy sauce
2 tablespoons sesame seeds
⅛ teaspoon salt
⅛ teaspoon pepper
1 green onion, chopped fine; use a good portion of the green
1 clove garlic, chopped fine
1 teaspoon peanut oil
1 tablespoon granulated sugar
1 teaspoon Accent

Using a very sharp knife, remove all the meat from the chicken. Cut into ⅛-inch thick slices about 2 inches square. Save the bones and skin to make soup. Add soy sauce to the chicken. Place the sesame seeds in an iron skillet and heat until the seeds begin to swell up and pop. Put the seeds in the bottom of a wooden bowl along with the salt and, using the back of a large spoon, crush them as fine as possible. Add the pepper, onion, garlic, peanut oil, sugar and Accent. Stir the chicken and the soy sauce into this mixture and let stand for 30 minutes.

Then put the mixture into a large skillet, cover, and cook over low heat until the chicken is tender. If it becomes too dry during the cooking time, add a little water. Serve at once, piping hot. Serves 4.

2 broilers, approximately 2 pounds each
¼ cup sesame seeds
3 tablespoons cooking oil
¼ cup soy sauce
¼ teaspoon pepper
2 scallions, sliced 1/16 inch thick (include a generous portion of the tender green part)
2 cloves garlic, chopped fine
2 tablespoons light brown sugar

Using a very sharp knife, remove all the meat from the chicken. (Save the skin, bones, giblets, etc, for soup. See Chapter #5.) Cut up the chicken into bite-sized portions. Set aside.

Place the sesame seeds and cooking oil in a skillet over moderate heat. Sauté the seeds until they are golden brown. Remove from heat and set aside to cool.

Using the back of a tablespoon, crush the cooled sesame seeds right in the oil in which they were browned. Then add the soy sauce, pepper, scallions, garlic and sugar. Mix the oil, seeds and flavorings with the bite-sized pieces of chicken. Set aside to marinate for 1 hour.

Arrange the pieces of chicken in the bottom of a shallow baking pan. Place under the broiler, about 6 inches away from the heat. After the exposed side of the chicken has turned golden brown, turn over all the pieces, using a broad spatula. Brown the other side. Serve at once, piping hot. This recipe may be accompanied with plain boiled rice or noodles. Serves 4.

JAPANESE CHICKEN AND GREEN PEAS

1 chicken breast
4 tablespoons peanut oil
½ cup onion, diced in ¼-inch squares
¾ cup boiling water with 1 tablespoon instant chicken bouillon dissolved in it
½ teaspoon Accent
½ teaspoon granulated sugar
1 teaspoon soy sauce
1 tablespoon cornstarch, dissolved in 3 tablespoons water
1 10-ounce package frozen baby peas, thawed to room temperature
2 tablespoons dry sherry or sake

Using a very sharp knife, cut all the chicken meat off the bones. Cut up the meat into ½-inch cubes.

Place the peanut oil in a large skillet over low heat. When it is hot, add the onions, and cook until they begin to get limp. Add the chicken and cook until it is firm and white. Add the water and bouillon. Add the Accent, sugar and soy sauce to the cornstarch and water. Stir well, then pour on the chicken. Cook over low heat for a few seconds until the sauce begins to thicken; stir constantly. Add the peas and sherry. Mix well, and cook a few seconds longer, until thoroughly heated. Serve at once, piping hot. Serves 4.

GREEN ASPARAGUS AND WHITE CHICKEN, JAPANESE STYLE

1 chicken breast
1½ cups cold water
12 young, tender asparagus spears
2 tablespoons peanut oil
2 tablespoons dry sherry or sake
1 teaspoon Accent
1 teaspoon sugar
1 teaspoon soy sauce
¼ teaspoon salt
1 tablespoon cornstarch

Using a very sharp knife, remove all the meat from the chicken bones. Cut the meat into ribbons ¼ inch thick by 1½ inches long. Set aside. Break up the chicken bones and put them in a saucepan with the cold water. Bring to a rolling boil; remove any froth that may gather. Turn the heat back to simmer, cover and cook for 30 minutes to extract broth.

Wash the asparagus spears under running water. Use only the tender portion; discard any tough pieces near the root. Cut the asparagus diagonally into 1½-inch lengths. Strain the broth and pour ¾ cup of it over the asparagus in a saucepan. Bring to a boil and cook for 10 minutes without covering. Drain, and discard the broth.

Heat the oil in a skillet over low heat; add the chicken and sauté until white and firm. Stir the sherry, Accent, sugar, soy sauce, salt and cornstarch into another ¾ cup of broth. Pour this over the chicken and continue to cook over low heat, stirring constantly until the mixture is transparent and thickened. Add the asparagus pieces; heat through and serve at once, piping hot. Serves 4.

JAPANESE STYLE CHICKEN BREAST #1

2 chicken breasts
2 tablespoons all-purpose flour
½ teaspoon salt
⅛ teaspoon white pepper
½ cup pancake flour
1 egg, beaten until lemon yellow
1 cup cold water
½ cup peanut oil
1 large lemon, cut into lengthwise wedges

Using a very sharp knife, remove the meat from the rib-cage and breastbone; keep the meat from each side of the breast in one large piece if possible. Dust the four pieces of meat with the flour, salt and pepper. Set aside on waxed paper for a few minutes.

Put the pancake flour in a bowl; alternately add the egg and the cold water. Beat with a slotted spoon or a whisk so that there are no lumps in the batter.

Dip each piece of floured chicken in the batter. Place the peanut oil in a skillet and, using very low heat, sauté the chicken until it is golden brown. Place the chicken on paper toweling for a few seconds after removing from the oil.

Cut each chicken breast crosswise into 1½-inch strips. Top each strip with a wedge of lemon. Serve piping hot. Serves 4.

JAPANESE STYLE BREAST OF CHICKEN #2

1 chicken breast
3 tablespoons soy sauce
1 teaspoon grated ginger root
¼ cup sake or dry sherry
1 teaspoon Accent
2 tablespoons peanut oil
2 tablespoons cornstarch

Using a very sharp knife, remove the meat from the chicken breast. Try to keep it in two pieces. Mix together the soy sauce, ginger, sake and Accent and pour over the chicken. Let stand for 45 minutes; turn the chicken over three or four times so that it is evenly coated and flavored.

Heat the peanut oil in a skillet; dip the chicken in the corn-starch and fry in the oil until it is an even golden brown.

Add a tablespoon of water, cover and cook over low heat until done; the thickest portion should be easily pierced with a fork.

Remove from the skillet and allow to cool. Slice into very thin slices and serve. Serves 2.

HAWAIIAN FLAIR CHICKEN

This recipe has to be made the day before.

2 2- to 3-pound broilers, cut in half lengthwise
1 cup of Bermuda onions, sliced thin
1 46-ounce can pineapple juice
½ cup rum
¼ cup peanut oil
½ cup soy sauce
¼ cup dry white wine
½ cup granulated sugar
¼ cup lemon juice
¼ teaspoon grated lemon rind
½ teaspoon ground ginger root
½ teaspoon salt
¼ teaspoon freshly ground pepper
1 cup mushroom buttons

Wipe the chicken, inside and out, with paper toweling. Place the chicken halves in a large, tightly covered bowl along with the onion slices. Mix the pineapple juice and rum together; pour it over the chicken. Put in the refrigerator for at least 24 hours.

Next day, pour off the pineapple-rum marinade and reserve. Mix together the peanut oil, soy sauce, wine, sugar, lemon juice, lemon rind, ginger salt and pepper. Shake vigorously, and set aside while you arrange the chicken in a large shallow baking pan. Distribute the onion over, under and around the chicken. Shake the oil mixture once more and pour over the chicken. Arrange the mushrooms around the chicken and put in a 325° F. oven for 1 hour.

Then add 1 cup of the rum-pineapple mixture to the chicken. Return to the 325° F. oven for 1 additional hour, or until the chicken is tender enough to pierce with a fork in the thickest portions. Serve with hot fluffy rice. If you want to go completely Hawaiian, garnish with ¾ cup toasted coconut chips.

CHINESE CHICKEN WITH BLANCHED WALNUTS

1 chicken breast
1 unbeaten egg white
2 cups English walnuts
6 tablespoons peanut oil
1 tablespoon dry sherry wine
1 teaspoon Accent
1 teaspoon sugar
1 teaspoon salt
¼ teaspoon powdered ginger root
3 tablespoons cornstarch
3 tablespoons soy sauce
¼ cup water

Using a very sharp knife, remove all the meat from the chicken bones. Cut the meat into ¾-inch cubes; put them in the unbeaten egg white. Stir and turn so that all is covered.

Place the walnuts in a saucepan and cover with cold water. Bring to a rolling boil for 2 minutes, then let stand for 1 minute longer. Drain the walnuts and remove the skins.

Place the peanut oil in a skillet over low heat. Add the walnuts and sauté over low heat until they begin to turn golden brown. Remove the nuts from the oil, then add the chicken-egg white mixture and cook over low heat until the chicken is lightly browned and firm.

Mix together the rest of the ingredients. Stir well and pour over the chicken. Cook for a few seconds, until thickened. Add the walnuts and continue to cook over low heat until thoroughly warmed through. Serve piping hot. Serves 4.

CHINESE CHICKEN WITH PINEAPPLE

1 chicken breast
½ teaspoon salt
½ teaspoon Accent
2 teaspoons granulated sugar
2 teaspoons soy sauce
2 tablespoons cold water
2 tablespoons cornstarch
6 tablespoons peanut oil
1 cup celery, diced in ½-inch pieces
¾ cup sweet onion, diced in ½-inch pieces
1 #311 can pineapple wedges (reserve ¼ cup of the juice)

Using a very sharp knife, remove the meat from the chicken breast; cut up into bite-sized cubes. Mix together the salt, Accent, sugar, soy sauce and cold water. Stir in the cornstarch and pour over the chicken. Let it marinate for 1 hour; turn frequently so that the flavors are blended.

Heat 3 tablespoons of peanut oil in a large skillet and then drain the chicken and place it in the oil. Save the leftover marinade for later. Sauté the chicken until it is golden brown, then remove from the oil and set aside.

Put the 3 remaining tablespoons of the oil in the skillet; heat, and add the celery and onion. Sauté until the celery and onion are glazed and transparent. Pour off any excess oil. Add the marinade, the pineapple juice and pineapple and turn up the heat slightly. Add the chicken and continue to cook until heated through. Serve, piping hot, with fluffy rice. Serves 6.

CHICKEN WITH CAULIFLOWER, CHINESE STYLE

1½ cups coarsely chopped cooked chicken meat
1 large cauliflower, broken into flowerets, or 3 packages frozen
  cauliflower
2 eggs, separated
½ teaspoon salt
1½ cups chicken broth
3 slices bacon, fried crisp and then crumbled

Cook the cauliflower in salted boiling water until you can pierce the thickest stems with a fork. Drain and set aside.

Beat the egg whites with a fork until they begin to get bubbly and frothy; add the salt and ½ cup of the chicken broth. Beat again. Add the chicken meat and stir well.

Bring the remaining cup of chicken broth to a rolling boil. Turn off the heat, and slowly pour in the egg and chicken mixture. Beat gently all the while you are combining these ingredients.

Beat the egg yolks until they are lemon yellow. Add them to the broth mixture; stir well. Turn on the heat again and cook for a few seconds. Stir in the cauliflower pieces and continue to cook for 5 minutes longer. Stir gently so that you do not break up the cauliflower. In this 5 minutes the mixture should just begin to thicken and become heated through. Place on a heated platter and sprinkle the fried bacon over the top. Serves 4.

CHINESE CHICKEN AND PEPPERS

1 3-pound fryer-broiler, cut into portion-sized pieces
¼ cup soy sauce
1 teaspoon salt
½ teaspoon Accent
1 teaspoon sugar
1 tablespoon cornstarch
½ cup peanut oil
1 cup green pepper, diced in ½-inch cubes
1 cup red sweet pepper, diced in ½-inch cubes
1 cup cucumber, diced into ½-inch cubes
1 cup stock made from the chicken bones

Using a very sharp knife, remove all the meat from the chicken bones. Cut it up into bite-sized pieces. Place the bones and skin from the chicken in a saucepan with 1 cup of cold water. Bring to a boil, and skim off any froth that may gather. Cover, turn back to simmer, and cook for 1½ hours.

Meanwhile, mix the soy sauce, salt, Accent, sugar and cornstarch. Pour this over the cut-up chicken and allow to marinate for 1½ hours. Turn the chicken over frequently so that the flavors are well blended. Drain, and save the marinade.

Heat the peanut oil in a large skillet and place the chicken in it. Sauté until the white meat is firm and tender. Remove the meat from the oil and set aside.

Add the green and red pepper to the oil in the skillet, and sauté until the green pepper begins to get transparent on the edges and is slightly glazed. Add the cucumber and cook for a few seconds longer.

Drain the stock off the chicken bones and add one cup of it to the pepper mixture. Add the remainder of the marinade. Stir well, and cook over low heat.

Add the chicken and continue to cook over low heat until the chicken is heated through. Serve at once, piping hot. Do not cover this dish during the cooking, as you will spoil the colors of the vegetables. Serves 4.

Variations:

Should you desire a thicker gravy to glaze the vegetables, stir
   1 tablespoon of cornstarch into the chicken broth before
   adding to the vegetables. Stir from time to time to prevent
   sticking.
Serve over fluffy boiled rice.
Serve over chow mein noodles.
Serve over boiled egg noodles.

At the last minute of cooking, stir in ½ cup of water cress cut into ½-inch segments.

Garnish with ½ cup of coarsely chopped pecans.

CHICKEN CHOW MEIN WITH FILBERTS

1 3-pound fryer, cut into portion-sized pieces
3 tablespoons butter
1 cup filberts, cut in halves
1½ cups water
1 cup diced onion
1½ cups celery, bias-sliced in ⅛-inch strips
¼ cup green pepper cut into ¼-inch cubes
¾ cup mushroom stems and pieces
1 #2 can bean sprouts
3 tablespoons soy sauce
2 tablespoons cornstarch dissolved in ¼ cup cold water
4 cups cooked hot fluffy rice

Place the chicken pieces and butter in a large skillet and sauté until golden brown. Remove chicken and set aside. Put the filberts in the remaining butter and sauté until they are golden brown. Remove the filberts and set aside. Put the water, onion, celery and green pepper in the skillet along with the chicken pieces, and simmer, covered, for 15 minutes, or until the chicken is tender and the celery is glazed and soft. Remove the chicken and set aside to cool so that all the meat can be removed from the bones.

After you remove the meat from the bones, cut it into bite-sized pieces and place it, along with the mushrooms, bean sprouts, and soy sauce, in the skillet again. Simmer for 5 minutes longer. Stir in the cornstarch and water and continue to simmer until the mixture thickens. Serve over the portions of hot rice; top with the filbert nuts. Serves 4.

Variation:

Use one #2 can chow mein noodles along with the rice.

CHICKEN AND ALMONDS, CHINESE STYLE

2 chicken breasts
¼ cup soy sauce
3 tablespoons cornstarch
1 teaspoon salt
1 teaspoon granulated sugar
8 tablespoons peanut oil
¼ cup boiling water with 1 teaspoon instant chicken bouillon dissolved in it
1 cup green celery, cut diagonally ⅛ inch thick
1 cup sweet onions, cut in ⅛-inch slices
1 cup bamboo shoots, drained and cut into ⅛-inch slices
1 cup toasted almonds
1 4-ounce can water chestnuts, drained and cut into ⅛-inch slices
¼ cup sake or dry sherry (optional)

Using a very sharp knife, remove all the meat from the chicken breasts. Slice into ribbons ¼ inch thick by ½ inch wide. Mix the soy sauce, cornstarch, salt and sugar together and pour over the chicken. Let them soak in this for at least an hour. Turn from time to time so that all is evenly flavored. At the end of this hour, drain, and save any of the marinade that is left.

Heat 4 tablespoons of peanut oil in a large skillet. Add the chicken meat and sauté over low heat until the meat is white and firm. Add the boiling water and bouillon and let simmer for about 10 minutes. Add the marinade and mix well.

In another skillet, heat the second 4 tablespoons of peanut oil. Add the celery and sauté until it is glazed around the edges. Remove the celery and then sauté the onions in the hot oil until they are limp and transparent. Remove the onions. Add the celery and onions to the chicken. Add the bamboo shoots, almonds and water chestnuts; mix all lightly and continue to cook over very low heat until warmed through. Do not cover, or the vegetables will lose their color. Just before serving, stir in the sake or sherry. Serve piping hot. Serves 6.

Variations:

Substitute toasted cashew nuts for the almonds.
Substitute toasted pecans for the almonds.
Substitute pine nuts for the almonds.

Substitute English walnuts for the almonds, but blanch them first by boiling in slightly salted water for 3 minutes. This will loosen most of their skins and take away some of the harshness of their flavor, which is apt to overwhelm the delicate chicken and vegetable flavors in the recipe.

CHINESE STYLE CHICKEN WITH RICE

3 cups diced, cooked, white chicken meat
3 cups long grain rice
3 cups water
2 chicken-flavored bouillon cubes
3 tablespoons butter
¾ cup diced fresh pork (pork steak meat is ideal)
4 scallions, cut into 1/16-inch pieces; include a little of the tender green
1 cup mushroom stems and pieces, either fresh or canned
4 tablespoons soy sauce
½ teaspoon salt
¼ teaspoon pepper
4 eggs
1 tablespoon thick cream

Place the rice, water and bouillon cubes in a large kettle with a tight-fitting cover. Bring to a rolling boil; stir a few times to loosen any rice that may have stuck to the bottom, then turn the heat back to simmer and continue to cook, covered, for ½ hour.

Meanwhile, melt the butter in a skillet and add the fresh pork. Sauté until the pork is browned and tender. Pour off half the fat and butter, and reserve. Add the chicken meat to the pork; add the scallions and mushrooms, and continue to sauté for 5 minutes longer. Add the soy sauce, salt and pepper. Mix very well. Pour this mixture over the cooked rice (no draining necessary) and continue to cook over low heat for 5 minutes longer.

Beat the eggs and cream together with a fork. Return the fat you have reserved to the skillet and scramble the eggs. Now stir the eggs into the chicken-rice mixture. Mix very well and serve at once. Serves 6.

CHINESE CHICKEN WITH MUSHROOMS AND SCALLIONS

2 chicken breasts
6 tablespoons peanut oil
1 4-ounce can bamboo shoots, cut into ⅛-inch slices
1 4-ounce can water chestnuts, cut into ⅛-inch slices
1 8-ounce can button mushrooms
1 teaspoon salt
1 teaspoon granulated sugar
1 teaspoon Accent
2 tablespoons dry sherry wine
1 tablespoon cornstarch
¼ cup soy sauce
¾ cup celery, cut diagonally
8 scallions, cut diagonally in ½-inch pieces; use a small
   portion of the tender green part, too
6 spinach leaves, cut in diagonal ribbons ¼ inch wide.

Using a very sharp knife, remove all the meat from the chicken breasts. Discard the skin and bones. Cut the meat into strips ¼ inch thick by 2 inches long. Put 3 tablespoons of the oil in a large skillet and sauté the chicken over low heat until it is white and tender; remove.

Mix together the bamboo shoots, water chestnuts and mushrooms. Combine the salt, sugar, Accent, sherry, cornstarch and soy sauce. Pour this over the bamboo shoot mixture. Let stand for 15 minutes.

Heat the 3 remaining tablespoons of oil in the skillet. Add the celery and scallions. Sauté over low heat until the celery is glazed and transparent. Add the bamboo shoot mixture and the sautéed chicken and continue to cook over low heat until thoroughly warmed through. Add the spinach just before serving. Do not cover at any time during cooking or the vegetables will lose their bright colors. Serve at once, piping hot. Serves 6.

Variations:

Dice 1 small, not overly ripe tomato into ¼-inch cubes and add this at the same time you add the spinach.
Sprinkle ½ cup toasted pecans, coarsely chopped, over the top just before serving.

CHINESE CHICKEN WITH CHESTNUTS

4 chicken legs, thigh and all
1 pound chestnuts
2 tablespoons peanut oil
2½ cups onions, sliced lengthwise ¼ inch thick
1 4-ounce can mushroom stems and pieces, drained
1 teaspoon salt
1 teaspoon Accent
1 teaspon sugar
¼ cup soy sauce
1 tablespoon dry sherry
¼ teaspoon powdered ginger root

Make a slit in the side of each chestnut with a sharp knife. Place the chestnuts in a saucepan and cover with water. Bring to a boil and cook for 20 minutes. Using a slotted spoon, remove three or four chestnuts at a time, and peel away the outer shell and the thin brown inner shell. Leaving the rest of the chestnuts in the hot water will make them easier to peel. After all are peeled, chop them coarsely and set aside.

Using a very sharp knife, remove all the meat from the chicken legs. Place the skin and bones in a saucepan with 2½ cups of water and bring to a rolling boil. Skim off any froth and turn heat back to simmer for 30 minutes. Cut up the chicken into cubes about 1 inch in size.

Place the peanut oil in a skillet over low heat. Add the chicken, and sauté until it is a light brown. Add the onions and continue to sauté until they are transparent and glazed. Strain the broth from the bones and skin and add it to the chicken and onions. Add the mushrooms, salt, Accent, sugar, soy sauce, sherry and ginger. Continue to cook over low heat, stirring frequently. Add the chestnuts and cook for 15 minutes longer. Serve piping hot. Serves 6.

Chapter XI

CHICKEN CASSEROLES

CHICKEN CASSEROLES ALWAYS used to seem to me an utter extravagance. However, with the low prices of today's chicken, I've overcome this notion.

Because I am basically lazy and very busy at the same time, casseroles are a favorite of mine. I always make enough for two meals, one to eat that day and the other to freeze and save for another time. Should you too want to follow this escape route from day in and day out cooking, just double up the recipes.

In this chapter you will find recipes that require fresh chicken and some where you can use leftover chicken. When money-saving sales come along on chicken, I sometimes go completely off the deep end and buy 15 or 20 of them. When I make a haul of this kind, I always cook three or four chickens ahead of time and then cube and freeze the meat for future casserole use. Not only is this good economy, but it saves time and work.

When cooking chicken for future casseroles, I use as little water as possible. The small amounts of broth that remain from cooking the chicken, I freeze in ice cube trays and then store in plastic bags. These "chicken-flavored ice cubes" are just wonderful for making gravy more flavorful. If you need just half a cup of chicken broth for some dish, all you have to do is melt a couple of cubes. Chicken broth can be purchased in cans, but I find the frozen cube method a lot more reasonable in cost.

Make some chicken casseroles and become a member of my lazy club.

CHICKEN SCALLOP

2 cups diced chicken, both light and dark meat
3 cups cooked potatoes, cut in ¼-inch slices
1 cup soft white bread crumbs
¾ cup grated Parmesan cheese
1 10-ounce can cream of chicken soup
1 cup milk
2 tablespoons butter or margarine

Spread 1 cup of the sliced potatoes over the bottom of a casserole. Mix together thoroughly the bread crumbs and cheese. Sprinkle a layer of this over the potatoes. Follow with a layer of chicken. Sprinkle the chicken with the cheese and crumb mixture. Add another cup of potatoes, cheese and crumbs and the remainder of the chicken. Follow this with a sprinkling of the cheese mixture, another layer of potatoes. Mix the soup with the milk and pour this over all. Sprinkle the top with the remainder of the crumbs and cheese. Dot with butter or margarine.

Bake in a 350° F. oven for 35 minutes, or until the top is golden brown. Serve at once, piping hot. Serves 6.

CHICKEN AND SHRIMP BAKE

2 cups diced cooked chicken, both light and dark meat
3 tablespoons butter
1 cup celery, diced in ¼-inch pieces
½ cup onion, diced in ¼-inch pieces
3 cloves of garlic, chopped fine
1 cup raw peeled deveined shrimp, cut into 1-inch pieces
1 8-ounce package frozen baby peas, thawed to room temperature
2 cups cooked fine egg noodles
½ teaspoon salt
¼ teaspoon pepper
½ teaspoon Accent
½ teaspoon coriander powder
½ cup chicken broth or ½ cup water with 2 chicken bouillon cubes dissolved in it
2 pimientos, cut into ¼-inch cubes

Melt the butter in a large skillet; add the celery, onion and garlic. Sauté until the onion is glazed and transparent. Add the shrimp and continue to cook until the shrimp turns pink and is firm. Remove from the heat.

Add the peas, chicken and egg noodles. Add the salt, pepper, Accent and coriander. Mix with a very light hand. Pour into a buttered casserole; pour the chicken broth over the top and then sprinkle the pimiento over all. Place in a 350° F. oven for 25 minutes. Serves 4.

Variations:

Add 1 cup of cubed ham for another flavor variation.
Use 1 8-ounce package niblet corn instead of the frozen peas.

CHICKEN DUMPLING PIE

1 3- to 4-pound fryer-broiler, cut up
2 cups cold water
1 teaspoon salt
¼ teaspoon pepper
2 hard-boiled eggs, peeled and sliced
7 tablespoons butter
2 cups all-purpose flour
3 teaspoons baking powder
½ teaspoon salt
⅔ cup milk
¼ cup half and half cream

Place the chicken pieces, water, salt and pepper in a sauce-pan with a tight-fitting cover. Bring to a rolling boil and skim away any froth that may gather. Reduce the heat to simmer, cover, and cook for 40 minutes, or until the thickest portions of the chicken can be pierced with a fork. Remove the chicken from the broth to cool. Measure the chicken broth; you should have at least two cups. If you do not, add water.

When the chicken is cool enough to handle, remove the skin and bones and discard. Cut the meat up into bite-sized portions. Divide the meat in half; place half of it in the bottom of a deep baking dish. Cover the meat with the sliced egg, dot with 2 tablespoons butter, and add 1 cup of broth. Set aside while you proceed to make the dumpling-crust mixture.

Sift the flour, baking powder and salt together twice. Cut the butter into the flour mixture until evenly mixed. Add the milk, a little at a time; mix after each addition of milk. After a soft dough has been formed, place on a floured board or pastry cloth and roll and pat until it is ½ inch thick. Cut strips about 1 inch wide by ½ inch thick and put half of them over the chicken and egg mixture.

Place the remainder of the cut-up chicken over these dough strips; add the second cup of broth. Cover this second layer of chicken with the remainder of the dough strips. Brush the tops of the dough strips with the cream.

Place in a 375° F. oven for 25 minutes, or until the top crust is puffed up and a crispy golden brown. Serve at once, piping hot. The delight of this dish is that the dough that covers the first layer forms into dumplinglike strips, while the strips that top the dish are crisp like pie topping. If your family likes both chicken and dumplings and old-fashioned chicken pie, this is an excellent dish. Serves 6.

Variations:

Add 1 10-ounce package of frozen peas to the top layer of chicken.

Add 1 10-ounce package of mushrooms frozen in butter sauce to the top layer of chicken. Diminish the second addition of broth by ½ cup.

CHICKEN CASSEROLE #1

1 5-pound stewing chicken, cut into serving pieces
1 teaspoon salt
¼ teaspoon pepper
½ cup all-purpose flour
1¾ cup milk
8 slices white bread with crusts removed, cubed into ¼-inch pieces
2 eggs, separated
1 cup mushroom stems and pieces
1 2-ounce can chopped ripe olives

Put the chicken pieces in a kettle and barely cover with water. Add the salt and pepper and cook until tender. Drain off the broth and place in the refrigerator to chill and solidify the fat that will rise to the top. Arrange the chicken in a 1½ quart buttered casserole.

Skim the fat off of the broth and put 3 tablespoons of it in the top of the double boiler over rapidly boiling water. Stir in the flour, then add 2 cups of chicken broth and the milk. If you do not have 2 cups of broth from boiling the chicken, add more milk. Stirring constantly, cook over the boiling water until thickened. Remove from the heat and stir in the bread cubes. Beat the egg yolks until they are lemon yellow; add a little of the hot broth mixture to them. Then add the yolks to the thickened broth. Mix well. Beat the egg whites until they stand in peaks. Fold them into the thickened sauce.

Pour this mixture over the chicken. Place in a 350° F. oven for 45 minutes. Ten minutes before serving, melt 1 tablespoon of the chicken fat or butter in a skillet; sauté the mushrooms until they are golden brown, add the chopped olives and mix well. Spread this mixture over the top of the casserole and continue baking. Serves 6.

CHICKEN CASSEROLE #2

1 2- to 3-pound frying chicken, cut up into serving pieces
2 tablespoons flour
½ teaspoon Accent
½ teaspoon salt
½ teaspoon paprika
¼ teaspoon black pepper
¼ cup onion, chopped fine
½ cup celery, chopped fine
3 tablespoons butter
½ cup water
1 cup half and half cream
2 cups broad cooked egg noodles

This recipe takes a large-sized casserole, for the pieces of chicken should all lie flat on the bottom. Arrange the chicken in the casserole; mix the flour, Accent, salt, paprika and black pepper and sprinkle over the chicken. Distribute the chopped onion and celery over all; dot with butter and bake in a 350° F. oven, uncovered, for 30 minutes.

Then add water and continue to bake, uncovered, for 25 minutes longer. Pour the cream over the chicken, cover tightly with aluminum foil and bake for a final 15 minutes at 350° F.

Arrange the cooked noodles on a platter, put the chicken on top and pour the cream gravy over all. Serve piping hot. Serves 6.

Variations:

Serve with fluffy rice instead of noodles.
Serve with chow mein noodles instead of boiled noodles.
Serve with mashed potatoes instead of boiled noodles.

CHICKEN CASSEROLE #3

1 5-pound stewing hen, cut up
1½ quarts water
1 teaspoon salt
¼ teaspoon pepper
1 8-ounce package fine egg noodles
1 10-ounce can golden mushroom soup
4 hard-boiled eggs, peeled and sliced
4 tablespoons butter
¾ cup bread crumbs

Put the chicken, water, salt and pepper in a kettle and bring to a rolling boil. Skim off any froth that may gather. Cover and cook over moderate heat for 1½ hours, or until the chicken is tender; then remove it and set it aside to cool. Reserve the broth in the kettle.

When the chicken is cool enough to handle, remove the bones and skin and discard. Cut up the chicken into bite-sized pieces.

Boil the egg noodles in slightly salted water according to the directions on the package. Drain and add them to 2 cups of the chicken broth. Add the mushroom soup.

In a deep casserole, place a layer of chicken pieces and sliced eggs. Follow this with a portion of the noodle mixture. Add another layer of chicken and eggs and again follow with the noodles. End with the noodles as the last layer. Melt the butter in a skillet, stir in the bread crumbs and sauté until the crumbs are thoroughly mixed with the butter and are beginning to turn slightly brown. Sprinkle the bread crumbs over the top of the casserole. Place in a 350° F. oven for 35 minutes, or until the crumb mixture is a rich golden brown. Serve at once, piping hot. Serves 6.

Variations:

Add 1 cup of mushroom stems and pieces along with the chicken layers.
Add 1 10-ounce package of frozen green peas along with the chicken layers.
Add 1 #2 can Chinese-style mixed vegetables, drained, to the chicken layers.
Top the casserole with 1 cup of chow mein noodles instead of crumbs.

CHICKEN STEW CASSEROLE

1 4- to 5-pound stewing hen, cut up; do not remove fat
6 cups cold water
1 teaspoon salt
¼ teaspoon pepper
1½ cups cooked rice (can be leftover rice)
4 eggs, beaten until lemon yellow
2 cups ½-inch bread cubes
2 pimientos, cut into ¼-inch pieces

For Gravy:

5 tablespoons flour
2 tablespoons lemon juice
½ teaspoon grated lemon peel
2 egg yolks, beaten until lemon yellow
1 cup mushroom stems and pieces, drained

Put the chicken in a kettle with the water, salt and pepper. Bring to a rolling boil and skim off any froth that may gather. Turn back to simmer, cover and continue to cook for 1 hour, or until the thickest portions of the chicken can be pierced with a fork. Remove the chicken from the broth and set aside until it is cool enough to handle. Skim the fat off the broth and set this too aside.

Remove the chicken from the bones and cut up into bite-sized pieces. To the chicken add the rice, eggs, bread cubes and pimientos. Add 3 tablespoons of the chicken fat and 3 cups of the reserved broth. Place in a greased casserole and bake for 50 minutes at 350° F. Then remove from oven and let stand for 10 minutes while you make the following gravy:

Melt ¼ cup of chicken fat in a saucepan. Stir in the flour and then add 2 cups of chicken broth. Cook, stirring constantly, until thickened. Add the lemon juice and lemon peel. Stir several tablespoonsful of the hot mixture into the beaten egg yolks, then add the egg yolks to the gravy. Stir until well blended. Add the mushrooms and heat a few seconds longer. Pour over the chicken. Serves 6.

CHICKEN WING CASSEROLE

Here is a delightful dish to serve when you find a bargain in packaged chicken wings. Be sure the wings are meaty, for there is no sense serving the scrawny variety. Who needs flavored chicken bones?

24 plump chicken wings with sharp tips removed
½ cup peanut oil
½ teaspoon Accent
½ teaspoon salt
¼ teaspoon pepper
½ cup honey
½ cup soy sauce
½ cup coarsely chopped sweet onion
1 cup mushroom stems and pieces with their liquid
1 cup uncooked instant rice
½ cup water

Pour the peanut oil in a large skillet and brown the chicken wings on all sides. Remove the wings from the oil and set aside. Mix together the Accent, salt, pepper, honey, soy sauce, onion, mushrooms, instant rice and water and pour into the skillet. Cook for a few minutes, stirring all the while; loosen any browned material left in the bottom of the skillet.

Place the browned chicken wings in a casserole with a tight-fitting cover. Pour the ingredients from the skillet over the wings. Cover tightly and bake in a 350° F. oven for 1 hour, or until the meat comes off the bones easily and the rice is puffed and separated. Serve piping hot. Serves 4.

Variation:

Substitute 1 cup loosely packed fine egg noodles for the rice.
 Add more water during cooking if the dish seems too dry.

BEAN POT CHICKEN

This is a recipe that my mother used to make on the ledge of our coal-fired furnace. Those days of the coal furnace are gone, but I have made this in my oven and the results are wonderful. For this recipe you must have an old-fashioned bean pot with a cover.

2 2- to 3-pound broilers, cut up into portion-sized pieces
1 teaspoon salt
¼ teaspoon pepper
1 teaspoon paprika
1 teaspoon Accent
¼ pound butter

Mix the salt, pepper, paprika and Accent. Place three or four pieces of the chicken in the bean pot, sprinkle a little of the mixed seasonings over it and follow with another layer of chicken until it is all packed in the bean pot. Place the butter on the top, then cover. Bake in a 275° F. oven for 3 hours, or until the thickest piece of chicken can be pierced with a fork. Place on a heated platter and serve piping hot. Serves 8.

This is delightful to take along on a picnic and serve right from the bean pot. It can be made the day before, refrigerated, then heated over a briquette fire at the campfire. It should not be placed directly over the coals, but off to one side so that it can warm slowly.

CHICKEN AND CHEESE CASSEROLE

1 5-pound stewing chicken, cut up into portion-sized pieces
4 cups cold water
2 tablespoons dehydrated onion
2 cups instant rice
2 cups American cheese, cut in ½-inch cubes
1 10-ounce can cream of mushroom soup
½ teaspoon salt
¼ teaspoon pepper

Place the chicken, cold water and onion in a saucepan and bring to a rolling boil. Skim off any froth that may gather on the top. Turn the heat back to simmer and cook for 1¼ hours, or until tender enough to pull the meat off the bones with a fork. Remove the chicken from the broth and set aside to cool.

Measure the broth, and bring up to 4 cups with additional water. Put the rice in the broth, bring to a rapid boil and then turn back to simmer and cover tightly. Cook at simmer, without stirring, for 15 minutes. Stir 1 cup of the cubed cheese, soup, salt and pepper into the rice. Remove the meat from the bones. Discard skin and bones. Mix half the chicken into the rice.

Place the rice and chicken mixture in a lightly buttered casserole. Top it with the remainder of the chicken and cheese. Put in a 350° F. oven for 30 minutes, or until the cheese has melted and turned golden brown. Serve immediately, piping hot. Serves 6.

CHICKEN AND HAM CASSEROLE

2 cups diced cooked chicken
1 cup cooked broad egg noodles
1 cup diced boiled ham
1 cup mushroom stems and pieces
1 canned pimiento, cut into ¼-inch pieces
2 tablespoons butter
2 tablespoons all-purpose flour
1 tablespoon granulated chicken bouillon
2 cups half and half cream
¾ cup buttered bread crumbs
½ cup grated Parmesan cheese

Mix together the chicken, noodles, ham, mushrooms and pimiento. Place in a buttered casserole and set aside while you make the sauce.

Melt the butter in a saucepan and stir in the flour. When it begins to get bubbly, add the bouillon and cream. Lower the heat and, stirring constantly, cook until the mixture is thickened and coats the spoon. Pour this over the chicken in the casserole.

Mix the bread crumbs and cheese. Sprinkle this over the mixture in the casserole. Place in a 350° F. oven for 30 minutes, or until the top is golden brown. Serve at once. Serves 4.

Variations:

Add 1 8-ounce package of thawed frozen peas to the chicken mixture.
Add 1 8-ounce package of thawed frozen niblet corn to the chicken mixture.
Eliminate the ham and use 3 cups of cooked chicken.
Substitute American cheese or mild Cheddar for the Parmesan.

SAUCED SOUTHERN ROAST CHICKEN

2 2- to 3-pound fryer-broilers, cut up into portion-sized pieces
1 cup all-purpose flour
1 teaspoon salt
¼ teaspoon pepper
2 teaspoons paprika
¾ cup peanut oil
1 cup chopped loosely packed parsley
1 cup green pepper, cut into ½-inch cubes
1 cup sweet onion, cut into ½-inch cubes
1 #2 can tomatoes
½ teaspoon mace
1½ teaspoons curry powder
½ teaspoon garlic powder
1 cup dried black currants
4 cups hot cooked fluffy rice
1 cup slivered toasted almonds

Put the flour, salt, pepper and paprika in a sack; shake up and down to mix well. Place 3 or 4 pieces of chicken at a time in the sack, and shake vigorously so that it is evenly covered. When all the chicken has been floured, place it on a sheet of wax paper for 15 minutes so that it absorbs the flour.

Heat the peanut oil in a large skillet. Brown the chicken evenly on all sides in the oil, then remove and set aside while you prepare the sauce.

In the oil left in the skillet, put the parsley, green pepper and onion. Sauté over low heat until the onion is transparent and glazed. Add the tomatoes, mace, curry powder and garlic powder and simmer over low heat for 20 minutes. Stir from time to time so that all the flavors are blended.

Pour the sauce into the bottom of a roaster with a tight-fitting cover. Place the chicken in the sauce, skin side down. Set in a 300° F. oven for 1 hour. Then turn the chicken over, skin side up, and continue to cook at 300° F. for another hour. Add the currants, making sure they are submerged in the sauce. Cover and continue to cook for 35 minutes longer.

Place the hot fluffy rice on the bottom of a deep platter, with the chicken on top. Pour the sauce and currants over all. Sprinkle the toasted almonds over the top. Serve at once, piping hot. Serves 6.

Variations:

If you like the flavor of currants, increase the amount according to taste and add an additional ½ cup of water per cup of currants.

Substitute 1 cup of coarsely chopped Virginia-style peanuts for the almonds.

Substitute 1 #2 can chow mein noodles for the almonds.

Substitute 1 cup of coarsely chopped toasted pecans for the almonds.

Substitute 6 chicken breasts, cut in half, for the whole chicken.

Substitute 6 chicken legs, thighs and all, for the whole chicken.

Substitute hot cooked fine egg noodles for the rice.

Substitute 1 cup of dark seedless raisins for the currants.

ROAST CHICKEN WITH GRAVY

1 5-pound roasting chicken, cut up into portion-sized pieces
1 teaspoon salt
1 teaspoon Accent
¼ teaspoon pepper
¾ cup all-purpose flour
½ cup melted butter or margarine
1 10-ounce can golden cream of mushroom soup
1 10-ounce can cream of chicken soup
1 cup milk
¼ cup parsley, chopped fine

Mix the salt, Accent, pepper and flour in a paper sack. Put two or three pieces of chicken in the seasoned flour and shake so that they are well covered. Repeat until you have flour-coated all of the chicken. Pour 4 tablespoonsful of the melted butter into the bottom of a baking dish. Put the pieces of chicken on top of the butter and then, using a pastry brush, coat the top side of each piece of chicken with butter. Place in a 350° F. oven for 35 minutes, or until the chicken has become golden brown.

Mix the mushroom soup, chicken soup, milk and parsley together. Pour this around the chicken. Reduce the oven heat to 300° F. and continue to bake for 2 hours. Turn the pieces of chicken over in the gravy several times during this period.

The chicken is done when the thickest portions can be pierced with a fork. Serve with fluffy hot rice. This is also delicious with plain mashed potatoes or baking powder biscuits. Serves 6.

CHICKEN BAKE

1 3-pound fryer, cut up into portion-sized pieces
½ cup melted butter
½ teaspoon salt
¼ teaspoon pepper
½ cup sliced onions
½ cup sliced celery
1 tablespoon minced parsley
¼ cup water
¼ cup brandy (optional)
¾ cup whipping cream

Put the chicken pieces and butter in a large skillet and brown evenly over low heat, then remove and set aside. Add the salt, pepper, onions, celery and parsley to the butter and sauté until the onions are transparent. Add the water, and scrape up any brown material from the bottom of the skillet.

Place the chicken in a baking dish with a tight-fitting cover and pour the onions, celery and broth over it. Cover and place in a 350° F. oven for 40 minutes, or until the thickest portions of chicken can be pierced with a fork.

Remove the chicken to a heatproof serving dish and put in the oven for a few seconds. To the broth left in the baking dish, add the brandy and cream. Stir well, and pour over the chicken pieces. Serve at once. Serves 4.

HUNGARIAN CHICKEN CASSEROLE

1 5-pound roasting chicken, cut up into portion-sized pieces
¼ pound butter or margarine
3 tablespoons flour
1½ cups dairy sour cream
1 cup mushroom stems and pieces
½ teaspoon salt
¼ teaspoon black pepper
¼ cup parsley, chopped fine
½ cup green pepper, chopped fine
5 scallions, cut up into ¼-inch pieces; use some of the green, too
½ cup milk
2 teaspoons paprika

Melt the butter in a large skillet and sauté the chicken until it is golden brown. Arrange the chicken pieces in a casserole with a tight-fitting cover. Return the butter remaining in the skillet to the heat and stir in the flour; cook until the flour turns golden brown. Remove from the heat and then stir in the sour cream. Blend until smooth. Stir in the mushrooms, add the salt, pepper, parsley, green pepper, scallions, milk and paprika. Blend until smooth and then pour over the chicken pieces in the casserole.

Cover the casserole and place in a 350° F. oven until the thickest pieces of chicken are tender enough to pierce with a fork. During the last 5 minutes of baking, remove the cover to allow steam to escape and to further brown the chicken. Serve piping hot. Serves 6.

CREOLE CHICKEN

1 3- to 5-pound roasting chicken, cut up into portion-sized pieces
1 teaspoon salt
¼ teaspoon pepper
1 teaspoon paprika
1½ cups coarsely chopped onion
1 cup packaged instant rice
1 #2 can tomatoes
1 medium-sized sweet red pepper
1 medium-sized green pepper
1 10-ounce package frozen okra pieces

Remove the fat from the chicken and place it in a large skillet over low heat to render. When it has completely rendered, place the chicken pieces in it and sauté them until they are golden brown. If the chicken itself does not possess enough fat for this, use butter to supplement. Sprinkle the salt, pepper and paprika over the chicken. Add the chopped onion, and continue to sauté until the onion is glazed and transparent.

Add the instant rice as it comes from the package, the tomatoes and red and green pepper. Bring to a slight rolling boil. Stir in the frozen okra and then place the entire mixture in a buttered casserole. Place in a 350° F. oven for 45 minutes, or until the thickest pieces of chicken can be pierced with a fork. Should the casserole become too dry during baking, add a little water. Serves 6.

CHICKEN IN GINGER ALE CASSEROLE

1 5-pound roasting chicken, cut up into portion-sized pieces
1 cup all-purpose flour
¾ cup corn oil
1 clove garlic, chopped
½ teaspoon salt
¼ teaspoon pepper
½ teaspoon Accent
2 cups ginger ale

Put the flour in a sack and place the chicken, 3 or 4 pieces at a time, in the sack and shake till it is thoroughly covered with flour. Heat the corn oil in a large skillet and sauté the chicken over low heat until it is golden brown on all sides.

Place the pieces of the browned chicken in a large casserole with a tight-fitting cover. Sprinkle the garlic, salt, pepper and Accent over the top. Pour in the ginger ale, cover and bake in a 350° F. oven for 1½ hours, or until the thickest portions of chicken can be pierced with a fork. Remove the cover the last 10 minutes of cooking to allow the steam to escape and to reduce the liquid. Serve at once, piping hot. Serves 5 or 6.

Chapter XII

STEWING CHICKEN

THERE ARE MANY methods of getting a chicken into a good stew. It can be done on top of the stove in a Dutch oven or a plain kettle, or it can be done in the oven in a heavy casserole or a shallow baking dish. Where the fine line of demarcation between stew and fricassee is drawn is often debatable. No matter which term is applied, chicken, when served in its own thickened juices, is delicious.

The joy of stewed chicken dishes is that they can be made ahead of time and rewarmed without any change in flavor. Naturally, refrigeration is an absolute must if you prepare chicken stews hours or days before you intend to use them.

When you are planning to stew a chicken, it is always wise to have the butcher cut it up into portion-sized pieces rather than try to cut it up at serving time. First of all, it takes less cooking time and heat if the chicken is precut. Second, the chicken makes a nicer appearance after cooking if it is in portion-sized pieces; often when you are trying to cut up a cooked whole stewed chicken, the meat slips from the bones and you end up with an unappetizing-looking mess.

Stewing chickens range in weight anywhere from 2½ to 5 or 6 pounds. Often a stewing chicken will contain more fat than other varieties; this excess fat should be removed with a sharp knife before cooking. If it is not removed, your stew will end up with pools of rich yellow chicken fat on its surface. The chicken fat you remove can be rendered over low heat and put to a variety of uses. Chicken fat is a delicious addition when frying potatoes; the fat can also be refrigerated and used when you are pan-frying a fryer-broiler chicken.

When you buy a stewing chicken in the 5-pound class be prepared to devote about 3 or 4 hours of slow cooking to it. After a chick has attained a weight of 5 or 6 pounds, you can rest assured that there is going to be a bit of toughness to the meat. This is not true in the case of capons. Due to minor surgery when young, capons do not get tough. Because of this built-in tenderness, capons usually lend themselves better to roasting than to stewing.

A heavy fryer, in the 3-pound class, lends itself well to certain stewing methods; you will find "fryers" specified in this chapter from time to time rather than stewing chicken. Heavy fryers, often hard to find, are a delight to stew.

Just because the label on your package reads "stewing chicken" does not mean that you have to serve it in a thickened gravy or sauce. Stewing chickens can be cooked ahead of time, slowly, in a small amount of water, and then used for sandwiches, salads, casseroles or creamed dishes. In this chapter we are going to deal with chicken stews; however, you will find other uses for cooked chicken in Chapters 8, 9 and 11.

CHICKEN STEWED IN CREAM—OVEN METHOD

1 2- or 3-pound fryer, cut up into portion-sized pieces
3 eggs, beaten until lemon colored
½ cup butter or margarine
2 cups flour
1 teaspoon salt
¼ teaspoon pepper
¼ teaspoon thyme
1½ cups light cream
2 tablespoons minced parsley

Dry the cut-up pieces of chicken with paper toweling and then dip them into the beaten eggs, making sure they are well covered with egg. Melt half of the butter in the bottom of a baking pan that is large enough for the pieces of chicken to lie side by side.

Put the flour, salt, pepper and thyme in a large paper bag and add the pieces of chicken, two at a time. Shake well so that the chicken is thoroughly covered with the seasoned flour. Put the chicken in the buttered baking pan; dot the chicken with the remaining butter. Place baking pan in a 450° F. oven for 30 minutes, or until the pieces start to get a crisp brown.

Reduce oven heat to 350° F. Pour the cream over the chicken and continue to bake for 30 minutes longer. Midway in this baking time, check to see if the chicken is getting dry; if so, add a little more cream. Do not turn over the chicken pieces during the baking, for the delight of this dish is the crispy portions combined with those that were submerged in cream. After removing from the oven, sprinkle with the minced parsley. Serve piping hot.

CHICKEN STEWED WITH MUSHROOMS—
OVEN METHOD

1 3-pound fryer, cut up into portion-sized pieces
½ cup flour
½ teaspoon salt
½ teaspoon savory
¼ teaspoon pepper
1 teaspoon paprika
¼ cup butter or margarine
1 cup mushroom stems and pieces with their liquid
1 10-ounce can cream of chicken soup
2 tablespoons sherry (optional)

Dry the chicken pieces well with paper toweling. Place the flour, salt, savory, pepper and paprika in a large paper bag and shake well to mix. Put the chicken into the bag with the flour and shake again so that all the pieces are coated.

Melt the butter in a baking pan large enough to hold all the chicken pieces laid out flat. Place the chicken in the melted butter and put into a 425° F. oven for 25 minutes, or until it is golden brown on the bottom. Turn each piece over.

Mix the mushrooms and their liquid with the soup and sherry and pour this over and around the chicken. Reduce oven heat to 375° F. and bake for 20 minutes longer, or until the soup is bubbly. Serve at once. Serves 6.

Variations:

Serve with fluffy mashed potatoes, using the excess soup as a gravy.
Serve with fluffy cooked rice, using the excess soup as a gravy.
Serve with broad boiled egg noodles, using the excess soup as a gravy.

CHICKEN POT PIE
OR CHICKEN STEW WITH BISCUITS

1 3- to 4-pound stewing chicken, cut up into portion-sized pieces
2 cups water
1 teaspoon salt
¼ teaspoon pepper
1 ¼-inch slice lemon
2 tablespoons cornstarch mixed with ¼ cup water
1 8-ounce package frozen mixed vegetables

Biscuit topping:

2 cups all-purpose flour
2 teaspoons baking powder
½ teaspoon salt
⅓ cup melted butter
¾ cup of milk

Put the chicken in a kettle with the water, salt, pepper and lemon. Bring to a rolling boil, and skim off any froth that may gather. Cover tightly and cook over low heat for 3 hours, or until you can pierce the thickest portions with a fork. Remove from heat and discard the lemon slice. Remove the chicken from the broth and set it aside until it is cool enough to handle.

Cut all the chicken meat from the bones and chop up into bite-sized pieces. Place the cut-up chicken in a buttered casserole dish. Measure the broth; if you have more than two cups, store the excess in the refrigerator to use for soup or gravy in the future. Place the two cups of broth over low heat and bring to a slow, rolling boil. Stir in the cornstarch and continue to cook and stir until thickened and transparent. Stir in the frozen vegetables just as they come from the package, then pour the thickened broth and vegetables over the chicken in the casserole.

Sift the flour, baking powder, and salt together three times. Cut the melted butter into the flour until all is well mixed and crumbly. Add the milk and mix with a light hand until a soft dough is formed.

Place the dough on a floured pastry cloth or board. Using a little additional flour on your fingers, pat until the dough is ½-inch thick. Cut into 2-inch circles, using a cookie cutter dipped in flour. Arrange the circles over the surface of the chicken mixture.

Bake in a 450° F. oven for 20 minutes, or until the biscuits have almost doubled in height and are golden brown. Serve piping hot. Serves 6.

Variations:

Use 1 8-ounce package of frozen peas in place of the vegetables.

Use 1 8-ounce package of frozen peas and carrots in place of vegetables.

Use 1 8-ounce package of frozen corn with pimiento in place of vegetables.

Use 1 8-ounce package of frozen French cut green beans in place of vegetables.

Add ¾ cup mushroom stems and pieces to the recipe, or use just mushroom buttons if you want to be super-fancy.

Substitute 1 cup of diced cooked ham for 1 cup of chicken; save the cup of chicken for a salad the next day.

Omit the biscuit topping and use 2 cups of fluffy cooked buttered rice instead. Lower the oven heat to 350° F. and bake for 15 minutes.

Omit the biscuit topping and use 2 cups of broad cooked buttered egg noodles topped with ½ cup buttered bread crumbs. Lower oven heat to 350° F. and bake for 25 minutes, or until crumbs are browned.

SKILLET CHICKEN STEW #1

1 3- to 4-pound stewing chicken, cut up into portion-sized pieces
½ teaspoon salt
¼ teaspoon pepper
3 tablespoons olive oil
1 cup coarsely chopped onion
1 cup instant rice
¼ teaspoon basil
¼ teaspoon orégano
1 #2 can tomatoes
3 tablespoons instant chicken bouillon
1 teaspoon granulated sugar
1 cup raisins
1 #2 can chicken broth

Wipe the pieces of chicken with paper toweling, sprinkle with salt and pepper. Heat the olive oil in a large skillet with a tight-fitting cover. Brown the chicken on all sides in the oil. Remove the chicken and set aside.

Add the onion to the oil and cook until it is glazed and transparent. Add the rice as it comes from the package. Add the basil, orégano and tomatoes; stir in the bouillon, sugar and raisins. Last, add the chicken broth. Bring all to a boil, add the pieces of chicken, then turn the heat to simmer. Cover and cook at simmer for 30 minutes. Then turn each piece of chicken over and cook another 30 minutes, or until the chicken is tender and the rice is fluffy. Leave the cover off in the last 5 minutes of cooking to let any liquid left in the bottom of the pan evaporate. Serve piping hot. Serves 6.

SKILLET CHICKEN STEW #2

1 3- to 4-pound stewing chicken, cut up into portion-sized pieces
1 cup self-rising pancake mix
1 teaspoon salt
¼ teaspoon pepper
½ cup peanut oil
1 10-ounce can cream of mushroom soup
½ cup half and half cream
1 cup Bermuda onion, sliced thin
¼ teaspoon thyme
⅛ teaspoon savory

Wipe the pieces of chicken with paper toweling. Place the pancake mix in a paper sack; add the salt and pepper and mix well by shaking up and down. Add the pieces of chicken a few at a time and shake well so they are thoroughly coated with flour.

Place the oil in a skillet with a tight-fitting cover. Brown each piece of chicken on both sides. Pour off any excess oil left after you are finished.

Mix the soup and cream and pour over the chicken. Arrange the onion over and around the chicken and then sprinkle with thyme and savory. Bring the mixture to a slow simmer, then cover and cook for 40 minutes, or until the thickest portions of the chicken can be pierced with a fork. Serve at once, piping hot. Serves 4.

Variations:

Add 1 10-ounce package of frozen peas 5 minutes before serving.
Add 1 10-ounce package of frozen niblet style corn 5 minutes before serving.

CHICKEN A LA KING

1 3- to 5-pound stewing chicken, cut up
3 cups water
4 tablespoons flour
1 teaspoon salt
¼ teaspoon pepper
⅛ teaspoon freshly grated nutmeg
1 2- to 3-inch diameter green pepper, diced into ¼-inch cubes
1 2- to 3-inch diameter sweet red pepper, diced into ¼-inch cubes
1 #4 can mushroom stems and pieces, drained
3 egg yolks, beaten until lemon yellow

Place the chicken in a saucepan with the water. Bring to a rolling boil and skim off any froth that may gather on top. Cover and cook at simmer for 1½ hours, or until the thickest portions can be pierced with a fork. Remove the chicken from the broth, and put the broth in the coldest part of the refrigerator so that the fat may rise to the top. Skim off the fat; you will need 4 tablespoonsful. If you do not get this much, augment it with margarine. Set chicken aside until later.

Put the chicken fat in a saucepan and melt over low heat; stir in the flour. When it begins to bubble, stir in 1½ cups of chicken stock. Continue to cook over low heat until thickened. Add the salt, pepper and nutmeg and continue to cook over low heat for a few minutes longer. Add the green and red pepper and continue to cook over low heat. Add the mushrooms and mix well.

Stir 3 tablespoons of the hot sauce into the egg yolks, then add the egg yolks to the sauce. Stir well, and continue to cook over very low heat.

The chicken may be added to the sauce in portion-sized pieces, or you can remove the meat from the bones and cube it into 1-inch pieces before adding. Cook for a few minutes longer so that all is warmed through. Serve piping hot. Serves 6.

Variations:

Serve in pastry shells or rosettes.
Serve over hot cooked fluffy rice.
Serve over broad cooked egg noodles.
Serve over baking powder biscuits.
Serve as an accompaniment to a mixture of small boiled potatoes and small boiled onions.

Serve in potato baskets which are obtainable in the bakery section of most supermarkets.

Serve over chow mein noodles.

Serve over mounds of hot shoestring potatoes.

CHICKEN AND CELERY ROOT POT

1 3- to 5-pound stewing chicken, cut up into portion-sized pieces
1 large celery root, about 1½ pounds
½ cup peanut oil or rendered fat from the chicken
2 cups sliced sweet onions, such as Bermuda, cut into ¼-inch thick pieces
½ teaspoon salt
¼ teaspoon pepper
1 8-ounce can tomato sauce
4 celery hearts, cut into ½-inch pieces, leaves and all

Soak the celery root overnight in cold water. (If it is not too dried out on the surface, several hours' of soaking will do.) Peel, and cut up into 1-inch cubes. Set aside.

Brown the chicken in the oil or chicken fat. Place in a roaster with a tight-fitting cover. Place the cubes of celery root and onion slices over the browned chicken. Sprinkle with the salt and pepper and add the tomato sauce. Distribute the celery heart pieces over all. Cover tightly and place in a 350° F. oven for 1 hour. Then turn the chicken pieces over, allowing some of the celery root, onions and celery pieces to fall into the sauce that has gathered in the bottom of the pan. If there is not at least ½-inch of juice in the pan at this time, add enough water to bring it up to ½-inch in depth. Cover again and continue to bake at 350° F. for 1 additional hour, or until the thickest pieces of chicken can be pierced with a sharp fork. Serve piping hot. Serves 6.

CHICKEN STEWED IN BEER

1 4- to 6-pound stewing chicken
¼ cup lemon juice
½ teaspoon Accent
1 teaspoon salt
¼ teaspoon pepper
1 12-ounce bottle beer or ale
½ cup onion, chopped fine
2 cloves garlic, chopped fine
½ small bay leaf
4 medium-sized potatoes, cut into quarters—scrub but do
  not peel
4 carrots, cut into circles ¼ inch thick
4 2- to 3-inch diameter onions
1 10-ounce package mushrooms frozen in butter sauce

For this recipe you need a roasting pan with a tight-fitting cover and large enough to hold the chicken upright. Dry the chicken inside and out with paper toweling; brush inside and outside with lemon juice. Sprinkle the Accent in the cavity and rub the outside of the chicken with pepper and salt. Place legs up in the roasting pan with the beer, onion, garlic and bay leaf. Place in a 350° F. oven for 1½ hours.

Turn the chicken over, breast side down; add the potatoes, carrots, onions and mushrooms. Cover again and return to the 350° F. oven for an additional 45 minutes. Serves 4 generously.

Chapter XIII

CHICKEN FOR THE GOURMET

IN MY PURSUIT of chicken recipes, I couldn't avoid some dishes that are absolutely in the gourmet class as far as flavor and cost of ingredients is concerned.

These dishes are saved for State Occasions. I also spring them on the family in February and March, when winter has us in its throes and spirits are dreary. It is amazing how a super-delectable dish will cheer the whole family on a particularly bad day.

A lot of dishes in this chapter use the choice white meat of the chicken. Others call for specific parts, like drumsticks, etc. If you want a little cache of gourmet pieces of chicken, it is wise to watch for supermarket sales. There are times when the price of chicken portions is incredibly cheap; that's when I buy them and freeze them for future use.

I find that frozen chicken works equally as well as fresh in these recipes. The only caution is: When freezing chicken, be sure that all of the air is out of the package and it is air tight. If there are leaks in the package or air inside it, you will lose a lot of your good chicken flavor. Improper freezing can turn a delectable piece of meat into something that resembles moist compressed sawdust.

Everyone enjoys a dish that is in the gourmet class. My difficulty is that I can never make enough to satisfy my hungry teenagers. This is one reason that the dishes in this chapter are served only on banner days. Many of the recipes contain brandy and wines; if you have teenagers, do not worry about the alcohol in these dishes, for most of it cooks away, leaving just a delectable union of flavors.

CHICKEN AMANDINE

3 chicken breasts, cut in half
1 cup all-purpose flour
¼ teaspoon rosemary
¼ teaspoon thyme
¼ pound butter
1 cup slivered almonds
1 clove garlic, chopped very fine
1 teaspoon A-1 meat sauce
1 10-ounce can chicken-rice soup
½ cup water
½ cup dry white wine
½ teaspoon salt
¼ teaspoon white pepper
½ teaspoon granulated sugar
1 cup mushroom stems and pieces

Put the flour, rosemary and thyme in a paper sack and shake to mix well. Place each chicken breast in this seasoned flour and shake the sack well so that each piece is thoroughly coated with flour. Melt the butter in a skillet and brown the chicken breasts on all sides. Remove from heat, then place the chicken breasts in a baking dish with a tight-fitting cover.

Return to the heat the remainder of the butter you used to brown the chicken. In it, sauté the almonds until they turn golden brown. Add the garlic, A-1 sauce, soup, water, wine, salt, pepper and sugar. Continue to cook over low heat for a few seconds, stirring all the while. Remove from the heat and stir in the mushrooms. Pour the entire mixture over the chicken. Cover and put in a 375° F. oven for 30 minutes, or until the thickest portions of the breast can be pierced with a fork. Serve with hot fluffy rice, cooked wild rice or boiled egg noodles. This is also excellent served on a piece of lightly toasted bread with a portion of the mushrooms and almonds distributed around the sides.

ROCAMBEAU CHICKEN
(Traveler's Chicken)

8 slices cooked chicken breast, approximately ½ inch thick
4 slices lean ham, approximately 4" x 4" x ½" thick
1 10-ounce can Cheddar cheese soup
8 bleached asparagus spears
½ cup grated mild Cheddar cheese

Place the ham slices in individual ovenproof serving dishes. You can also use a baking sheet if you do not have enough dishes. Spread each slice of ham with a heaping tablespoonful of soup. Top this with two slices of chicken breast. Again coat the chicken with a heaping tablespoonful of soup. Place two of the asparagus spears on top. Sprinkle with a portion of the grated cheese. Place in a 400° F. oven for 15 minutes, or until the cheese has melted and is bubbly. Serve at once, piping hot. If you like the flavor of browned cheese, put under the broiler for a few seconds until the cheese is crusty and brown. Serves 4.

CHICKEN BREASTS AND TIPSY MUSHROOMS

4 chicken breasts, cut in halves
¼ pound butter
1 pound 1-inch diameter fresh mushrooms
½ teaspoon salt
¼ teaspoon seasoned pepper (available in the spice section of most supermarkets)
2 tablespoons dehydrated parsley
¾ cup dry white wine, such as Rhine or sauterne
¾ cup dry vermouth
1 cup flour
¼ teaspoon thyme
¼ teaspoon savory
1 teaspoon garlic powder

Melt the butter in the bottom of a saucepan. Wash the mushrooms in lukewarm water and cut off any parts of the stems that are too large and dark in color. Drain the mushrooms thoroughly, then place them in the melted butter over moderate heat. Add the salt, pepper and parsley and sauté for 15 minutes, or until the cap side of the mushrooms begins to brown. Pour off the excess butter into another frying pan and reserve. Add the white wine and vermouth. Cover and cook over low heat for 15 minutes longer.

Mix the flour, thyme, savory and garlic powder together in a paper sack. Shake till thoroughly mixed. Place the chicken breasts in this seasoned flour and shake well until they are completely covered. In the reserved butter, sauté the chicken until it is golden brown. If necessary, add a little more butter. Place the chicken in a casserole with a tight-fitting cover. Pour the mushrooms in their wine sauce over the chicken. Place in a 325° F. oven for 25 minutes, or until the thickest portions of the breast are tender enough to pierce with a fork. Serve piping hot. Serves 4.

CHICKEN LIVERS WITH WILD RICE

1 pound chicken livers, cut in halves
¼ cup butter
½ cup diced raw bacon, cut into ¼-inch pieces
3 scallions, white portion only, sliced paper thin
¾ cup celery, cut diagonally ⅛-inch thick
1 cup mushroom buttons
3 pimientos, cut into ¼-inch cubes
3 cups cooked wild rice, cooked according to package
    directions
½ teaspoon salt

Place the butter and bacon cubes in a skillet over low heat.
Sauté the bacon until it is crisp and golden brown, then remove and set aside. Put the chicken livers in the butter and
bacon fat; sauté until tender. Remove the livers and set aside.

Place the scallions and celery in the butter left in the skillet,
and sauté them until the celery is transparent and tender. Return the bacon and livers to the skillet; add the mushrooms
and pimiento; cook for 5 minutes longer, or until warmed
through. Stir in the wild rice and salt. Serve at once. Serves 4.

If you want to prepare this dish ahead of time, make according to directions, then put in a well-buttered casserole. Place
in a 350° F. oven for 20 minutes, or until warmed through.

Variations:

Add 1 10-ounce can of cream of chicken soup, heat through
    and serve over toast wedges.
Add 1 10-ounce can of cream of mushroom soup, heat through
    and serve over toast wedges.
Add 1 10-ounce can of cream of celery soup, heat through
    and serve on toast wedges.

CHICKEN AND MUFFINS

2 large chicken breasts
1 teaspoon salt
1 teaspoon Accent
¼ teaspoon pepper
½ teaspoon cayenne pepper
2 English muffins
¼ cup melted butter
½ cup whipping cream, unwhipped

Using a very sharp knife, remove the white meat from each side of the bones of the chicken breast; take great care to keep each piece of meat whole and firm. Sprinkle the four pieces of meat with the salt, Accent, pepper and cayenne. Set aside while you prepare the muffins.

Cut the muffins in halves so that you have two equal circles from each. Place the muffin halves, cut side up, under the broiler until they are a delicate golden brown. Brush each half liberally with melted butter.

Put the muffins, toasted side up, in a baking dish with a tight-fitting cover. Place a piece of the chicken breast on each half. Brush the chicken with the unwhipped cream. Cover tightly and bake in a 350° F. oven for 30 minutes. Then brush again with the unwhipped cream, cover again, and continue baking for another 15 minutes. Serve piping hot. Chicken breasts made in this manner are a wonderful companion to a tasty mixed green salad. Serves 4.

CHILI CHICKEN

3 chicken breasts, cut in halves
¼ pound butter
2 cloves garlic, chopped fine
½ teaspoon seasoned pepper (found in the spice sections of supermarkets)
3 teaspoons chili powder
½ cup lemon juice
¼ teaspoon grated lemon rind
3 teaspoons Worcestershire sauce
1 16-ounce can peach halves, drained

Melt the butter in a saucepan. Add the garlic, seasoned pepper, chili powder, lemon juice and lemon rind and the Worcestershire sauce. Mix all very well.

Place the chicken breasts in a buttered casserole with a tight-fitting cover. Pour the flavored butter over the chicken, cover and place in a 350° F. oven for 45 minutes, or until the thickest portions of the breast can be pierced with a sharp fork.

Arrange the peach halves around the chicken. Spoon a little of the gathered juice over each peach half. Place under the broiler for 5 minutes, or until the chicken is golden brown and the peaches are warmed through. Serve at once, piping hot. Serves 6.

CHICKEN BREAST WITH CHIVES

3 chicken breasts, cut into halves
¼ pound butter
½ cup brandy
½ cup chopped chives
¼ cup chopped parsley
¼ teaspoon thyme
¼ teaspoon savory
½ teaspoon salt
½ teaspoon Accent
¼ teaspoon pepper
¾ cup dry sauterne
¾ cup whipping cream, unwhipped

Dry the chicken breasts well with paper toweling. Melt the butter in a large skillet. Over low heat, brown the chicken breasts on all sides. Pour the brandy over the chicken and light it. Shake the pan back and forth while the brandy is burning. As soon as the flame goes out, add the chives, parsley, thyme, savory, salt, Accent, pepper and sauterne. Continue to cook over low heat with the pan tightly covered for 1 hour, or until the thickest part of the chicken can be pierced with a fork.

Place the chicken on a heated platter in a 250° F. oven while you prepare the gravy. To the butter and browned granules left in the pan, slowly add the cream. Cook over low heat, stirring constantly until it is blended thoroughly and heated through. Pour over the hot chicken. Serve at once. Serves 6.

CHICKEN HAUT SAUTERNE

2 2- to 3-pound broilers, cut up into quarters or portion-
    sized pieces
½ cup melted butter
2 cloves garlic, chopped fine
1 teaspoon salt
¼ teaspoon pepper
1 teaspoon Accent
2 or 3 tablespoons paprika
2 cups Haut Sauterne wine

Wipe the chicken pieces with paper toweling. Place the garlic in the butter and let stand for a few minutes so that the flavors can unite.

Put the pieces of chicken, skin side down, in a large shallow baking dish. Brush each piece of chicken with the garlic-flavored butter. Mix the salt, pepper and Accent together and sprinkle over the chicken. Liberally sprinkle the chicken with paprika. Each piece should look red with paprika. Cover the baking dish with a large piece of aluminum foil and place in a 350° F. oven for 30 minutes.

Then turn the chicken over and, using a pastry brush, brush each piece with the melted butter gathered in the bottom of the pan. Re-cover with foil and return to the 350° F. oven for another 30 minutes. During this period, baste once or twice with the butter gathered in the bottom of the pan.

Remove the aluminum foil and pour the wine over the chicken. Continue to bake at 350° F. for another 30 minutes. During this time, baste the chicken frequently with the wine and butter gathered in the bottom of the pan. Test for doneness with a sharp fork. Serve piping hot. Serves 6.

CHICKEN LIVER PÂTÉ

1 pound chicken livers
1 cup unsalted butter
¾ cup onion, coarsely chopped
4 hard-boiled eggs
¼ teaspoon black pepper
½ teaspoon salt

Put the butter and chicken livers in a saucepan and sauté over very low heat until the livers are tender. Do not brown them. Remove the livers from the butter and set aside.

Place the onion in the butter remaining in the saucepan and sauté them until they are soft.

Using the fine blade on your meat grinder, grind the chicken livers alternately with a few spoons of the cooked onions and the butter. Then grind up the eggs.

Add the pepper and salt to the chicken livers and eggs. Beat with a wooden spoon until the pâté is light and fluffy. Serve by placing in a mound in the middle of a tray surrounded with rye crackers, white crackers, toast rounds.

CHICKEN BREAST BAKE

6 fryer-broiler chicken breasts, cut in halves
1½ cups all-purpose flour
½ teaspoon thyme
½ teaspoon pulverized sage
½ teaspoon savory
½ teaspoon salt
¼ teaspoon pepper
¼ pound butter, melted
1½ teaspoons Accent
1½ teaspoons paprika

Mix the flour, thyme, sage, savory, salt and pepper together in a paper sack. Drop each half of chicken breast in the bag; shake it well so that it is completely covered with the flour mixture.

Place 4 tablespoons of the butter in the bottom of a shallow baking pan big enough to accommodate all the pieces of chicken lying flat. Put the chicken breasts, skin side down, in the pan; sprinkle with half the Accent and half the paprika. Reserve the rest for the breast side of the chicken after it has been turned over.

Place in a 350° F. oven for 25 minutes. Then turn each piece of chicken over so that the skin side is up. Sprinkle the remainder of the melted butter over it, then the remainder of the Accent and paprika. Return the chicken to the 350° F. oven for 25 minutes longer, or until the breasts are golden brown and can easily be pierced with a sharp fork at the thickest portion. Serves 6.

CHICKEN BREAST SUPREME

4 whole chicken breasts, cut in half lengthwise
Juice of 2 lemons
1 teaspoon Accent
1 teaspoon salt
¼ teaspoon pepper
¾ cup all-purpose flour
½ cup unsalted butter
½ teaspoon dill seed
½ cup brandy
1 10-ounce can cream of mushroom soup
3 tablespoons sherry
1 tablespoon minced parsley

Marinate the chicken breasts in the lemon juice for 2 hours

or overnight. Remove them from the juice and reserve it until later. Sprinkle each breast with the Accent, salt and pepper.

Place the flour in a large sack and put one breast at a time in it. Shake well so that all sides of the chicken are coated. Melt the butter in the skillet and slowly brown the breasts on both sides. Sprinkle dill seed over the top; add the lemon juice and brandy, and cover tightly. Continue to cook over very low heat for 30 minutes, or until the thickest part can be pierced with a fork.

Heat the mushroom soup in a double boiler just as it comes from the can. Add the sherry and parsley. Place the chicken breasts on a heated platter and pour the mushroom soup mixture over the top. Serves 4.

OYSTER-CHICKEN GUMBO

4 chicken breasts
½ cup diced lean bacon
1 cup diced lean ham
½ cup diced onion
2 tablespoons parsley, chopped fine
⅛ teaspoon thyme
6 cups boiling water
1 cup sliced okra—frozen, not canned
1 bay leaf
¼ teaspoon pepper
½ teaspoon salt
2 dried red chili peppers
1 quart stewing oysters with their liquid
2 cups hot cooked fluffy rice

Place the chicken breasts and bacon in a large soup kettle and sauté until the bacon is crisp and the breasts are golden brown. Turn the chicken frequently so that it browns evenly. Add the onion and continue to sauté until it becomes transparent. Add the parsley, thyme, water and okra; bring to a rolling boil and skim off any froth that may gather. Add the bay leaf, pepper, salt and chili peppers. Turn the heat down to simmer and cook for 1 hour.

Remove the chicken breasts from the soup; cut the white meat from the bones. Return the pieces of meat to the soup. Add the oysters and their liquid to the soup and continue to cook for 5 minutes longer, or until the edges of the oysters begin to curl. Remove the chili pepper pods.

Place ½ cup of the hot rice in each soup bowl and top with a portion of the gumbo. Serves 4.

STUFFED CHICKEN BREASTS WITH MUSHROOMS

4 chicken breasts
1 teaspoon salt
½ teaspoon Accent
¼ teaspoon pepper
4 cups fluffy cooked rice
4 hard-boiled eggs, coarsely chopped
¼ cup celery, chopped fine
¼ cup parsley, chopped fine
¼ teaspoon thyme
¼ teaspoon marjoram
¼ teaspoon savory
½ cup warm water with 2 tablespoons instant chicken bouillon dissolved in it
¼ cup melted butter
2 10-ounce packages mushrooms frozen in butter sauce
½ cup half and half cream

Rub the ribcage of the chicken with a portion of the salt, and sprinkle with Accent. Rub the outside with the remaining salt and the pepper.

Mix together the rice, eggs, celery, parsley, thyme, marjoram, savory and water with bouillon. Add the butter and then fill each breast with ¼ of the mixture. If they bulge a little, don't worry. Fasten the lower part of the breast together with skewers or by sewing with string.

Put the breasts on the bottom of a buttered baking dish; surround them with the mushrooms and butter sauce. Place in a 350° F. oven for 35 minutes, or until the thickest portions can be pierced with a fork. Baste several times with some of the butter sauce surrounding the chicken. If necessary, brown for a few seconds under the broiler. Serves 4 generously.

CHICKEN DE CREME

4 chicken breasts
½ teaspoon salt
½ cup melted butter
1 10-ounce can golden cream of mushroom soup
1 cup dairy sour cream
1 teaspoon Accent
1 cup mushroom buttons

Using a very sharp knife, remove the meat from the rib-cage in two complete pieces if possible. Rub the chicken with the salt and set aside for 15 minutes.

Melt the butter in a large skillet. Brown the chicken breasts in the butter.

Place the chicken in a baking tin; mix the soup and sour cream together until completely blended. Pour this over and around the chicken. Sprinkle with Accent. Place in a 375° F. oven for 30 minutes, or until the chicken is slightly browned and fairly tender when pierced with a sharp fork. Distribute the mushrooms around the chicken and return to the oven for an additional 15 minutes.

Serve with baking powder biscuits or fluffy hot rice. If you want to be especially festive, garnish with ½ cup toasted almond chips. Serves 4.

CHICKEN BREAST BARBECUE

4 chicken breasts, cut in halves
½ cup soft butter
¼ cup lemon juice
½ cup cream of mushroom soup
¼ teaspoon powdered mustard
Dash of cayenne
½ teaspoon salt
¼ teaspoon black pepper
½ teaspoon smoke flavoring (liquid type is best)
½ teaspoon paprika

Whip the butter with a whisk or slotted spoon until creamy. Add the lemon juice and continue beating. Add the mushroom soup, mustard, cayenne, salt, pepper, smoke flavor and paprika and continue to beat for a few seconds longer.

Using a pastry brush, liberally cover each piece of chicken with the butter mixture. Let stand at room temperature for 30 minutes.

Put the chicken breasts in a shallow baking pan and cover with aluminum foil. Set in a 350° F. oven for 30 minutes. Then remove foil and baste the chicken breasts with the juices that have gathered in the bottom of the pan. Continue to bake without covering for an additional 15 minutes, or until the breasts are tender and a delicate golden brown. Serves 4.

CHICKEN AND SWEETBREADS WITH SHERRY

1 raw chicken breast from a fryer-broiler
2 sections of sweetbreads
1 tablespoon lemon juice
6 tablespoons butter
½ teaspoon salt
¼ teaspoon pepper
1 scallion, white portion only, chopped fine
4 tablespoons dry sherry
¾ cup button mushrooms
2 egg yolks, beaten until lemon yellow
1 cup heavy whipping cream
½ teaspoon paprika
¼ teaspoon curry powder (optional)

Boil the sweetbreads in slightly salted water until they are firm and white. Remove from the heat and rinse in cold running water. Set them aside in cold water to which you add 1 teaspoon of lemon juice. Set aside while you prepare the chicken.

Using a very sharp knife, remove the meat from the ribcage of the chicken. Slice ⅛-inch thick. Melt the butter in a skillet with a tight-fitting cover. Place the sliced chicken in the butter and sauté until it is curled and the edges begin to brown.

Peel away the membrane from the cooled sweetbreads, then slice them ⅛-inch thick. Add the sweetbreads to the chicken and continue to sauté over low heat for a few minutes. Add the salt, pepper, and onion. Add the wine, stir well and cover. Cook over very low heat for 8 minutes. Add the mushrooms and cook for 5 minutes longer.

Add the remainder of the lemon juice to the egg yolk; stir well, then add 3 tablespoonsful of the whipping cream. Stir this mixture into the sweetbreads and chicken. Stir again, making sure you bring up any browned material from the bottom of the pan. Pour into a buttered baking dish. Whip the rest of the whipping cream until it stands in peaks. Carefully fold in the paprika and curry powder. Using a rubber spoon, spread this flavored whipped cream over the sweetbreads and chicken. Place in the broiler, about 6 inches away from the heat, until the cream glazes over the meat. Serve at once, piping hot. Serves 4.

INDEX

A

Arroz con Pollo, 75

B

Baked Broilers with Stuffing, 28
Baked Chicken Dinner in One Pan, 30
Baked Chicken Dinner with a Zip, 35
Barbecued Broilers #2, 21
Barbecued Broilers #4, 22
Barbecued Broilers #5, 23
Barbecued Broilers #6, 24
Barbecued Broilers #7, 24
Barbecued Broilers #8, 25
Bean Pot Chicken, 144
Broilers Baked in Wine, 27
Broilers Chasseurs, 29
Broilers in Orange Sauce, 26
Broilers with Mushrooms, 26
Broiling chicken, 19
Broth, making and freezing of, 48, 111, 136
Buttermilk Fried Chicken, 12

C

Canned chicken, 10
Capons, 9, 31, 47, 61, 151
Casseroles
  Bean Pot Chicken, 144
  Chicken and Cheese Casserole, 144
  Chicken and Ham Casserole, 145
  Chicken and Shrimp Bake, 137
  Chicken Bake, 148
  Chicken Casserole #1, 139
  Chicken Casserole #2, 140
  Chicken Casserole #3, 141
  Chicken Dumpling Pie, 138
  Chicken in Ginger Ale Casserole, 150
  Chicken Scallop, 136
  Chicken Stew Casserole, 142
  Chicken Wing Casserole, 143
  Creole Chicken, 149
  Hungarian Chicken Casserole, 148
  Roast Chicken with Gravy, 147
  Sauced Southern Roast Chicken, 146
Cheese Pinwheels and Chicken, 110
Chicken a la King, 158
Chicken-Almond Salad Bowl, 119

Chicken Amandine, 162
Chicken and Almonds, Chinese Style, 132
Chicken and Broccoli Bake, 107
Chicken and Celery Root Pie, 159
Chicken and Cheese Casserole, 144
Chicken and Chip Casserole, 104
Chicken and Chives Sandwiches, 67
Chicken and Ham Casserole, 145
Chicken and Jellied Tongue Sandwiches, 66
Chicken and Muffins, 165
Chicken and Parmesan Sandwiches, 71
Chicken and Shrimp Bake, 137
Chicken and Sweetbreads with Sherry, 172
Chicken and Walnut Salad, 114
Chicken and Walnut Sandwiches, 68
Chicken Bake, 148
Chicken-Banana-Orange Medley, 109
Chicken Bone Soup from Roast Chicken Bones, 51
Chicken Booyah, 58
Chicken Breast Bake, 168
Chicken Breast Barbecue, 171
Chicken Breasts and Tipsy Mushrooms, 163
Chicken Breast Supreme, 168
Chicken Breasts with Chives, 166
Chicken Broth, 48
Chicken Burgers Supreme, 62
Chicken Cacciatore #1, 78
Chicken Cacciatore #2, 78
Chicken Cacciatore #3, 79
Chicken Cacciatore #4, 80
Chicken Cacciatore #5, 80
Chicken Casserole #1, 136
Chicken Casserole #2, 140
Chicken Casserole #3, 141
Chicken Castillane, 76
Chicken Chow Mein with Filberts, 131
Chicken-Corn Chowder, 49
Chicken Croquettes, 98
Chicken Curry, 122
Chicken de Creme, 170
Chicken Dumpling Pie, 138
Chicken Gizzards with Herb Rice, 100
Chicken Gumbo, 59
Chicken, Ham and Egg Sandwiches, 68
Chicken Hash Patties in Buns, 64

Chicken Haut Sauterne, 166
Chicken in Ginger Ale Casserole, 150
Chicken Legs, Oriental Style, 122
Chicken Liver Paté, 167
Chicken Liver Sandwich Spread, 69
Chicken Livers Smothered in Onions, 93
Chicken Livers with Wild Rice, 164
Chicken Loaf for Rye Bread Sandwiches, 65
Chicken 'N Cheese Burgers, 65
Chicken 'N Peas, 105
Chicken Patties and Celery Root, 108
Chicken, Peas and Cheese, 111
Chicken Pot Pie, 154
Chicken-Olive Salad, 113
Chicken Salad, 112
Chicken Salad Supreme, 117
Chicken Salad with Fruit, 113
Chicken Salad with Hazelnuts, 118
Chicken Scallop, 136
Chicken Stew Casserole, 143
Chicken Stewed in Cream—Oven Method, 152
Chicken Stewed in Beer, 160
Chicken Stewed with Mushrooms, 153
Chicken Stuffed with Rice, 32
Chicken Tetrazzini, 83
Chicken-Vegetable Soup, 60
Chicken Wing Casserole, 143
Chicken with Cauliflower, Chinese Style, 129
Chili Chicken, 165
Chinese Chicken and Peppers, 130
Chinese Chicken with Blanched Almonds, 128
Chinese Chicken with Chestnuts, 135
Chinese Chicken with Mushrooms and Scallions, 134
Chinese Chicken with Pineapple, 128
Chinese Style Chicken with Rice, 133
Cranberry and Chicken Salad, 114
Creamed Chicken Supreme, 96
Cream of Chicken Soup Supreme, 50
Creole Chicken, 149

D

Dixie Chicken Salad, 115

E

East Indian Chicken Delight, 86
Egg Drops for Chicken Soup, 51

F

Far Eastern Chicken, 89

Fat from chicken, 48, 151
Freezer Tray Chicken Salad, 115
French Bean and Chicken Salad, 119
Fried Chicken Amandine, 15
Fried Chicken with Pineapple and Tomatoes, 14
Frozen Chicken, 10, 92, 161
Frying chicken, 11

G

Garlic Flavored Fried Chicken, 13
Golden Chicken Soup—Jewish Style, 54
Golden Dough Bits or Farfel, 56
Gourmet dishes
    Chicken Amandine, 162
    Chicken and Muffins, 164
    Chicken and Sweetbreads with Sherry, 172
    Chicken Breast Bake, 168
    Chicken Breast Barbecue, 171
    Chicken Breasts and Tipsy Mushrooms, 163
    Chicken Breast Supreme, 168
    Chicken Breast with Chives, 166
    Chicken de Creme, 170
    Chicken Haut Sauterne, 166
    Chicken Liver Paté, 167
    Chicken Livers with Wild Rice, 164
    Chili Chicken, 165
    Oyster-Chicken Gumbo, 169
    Rochambeau Chicken, 162
    Stuffed Chicken Breasts with Mushrooms, 170
Green Asparagus and White Chicken, Japanese Style, 125
Guatemala Chicken, 91

H

Hawaiian Chicken with Coconut, 87
Hawaiian Flair Chicken, 127
Hot Chicken and Veal Loaf Sandwiches, 64
Hot Chicken Salad #1, 116
Hot Chicken Salad #2, 116
Hot Chicken Sandwiches Supreme, 66
Hungarian Chicken Casserole, 148
Hush-Puppy Fried Chicken, 14

I

Italian Chicken and Green Peppers, 84
Italian Chicken Bake, 81
Italian Chicken with Golden Sauce, 82
Italian Egg and Chicken Broth, 53
Italian Egg Fluff, 52
Italian Style Chicken Soup, 52

J

Japanese Chicken and Green Peas, 124
Japanese Style Breast of Chicken #1, 126
Japanese Style Chicken Breast #2, 126
Jellied Chicken Loaf for Sandwiches, 70
Jellied Chicken Salad, 118

K

Korean Style Chicken #1, 123
Korean Style Chicken #2, 124

M

Maryland Fried Chicken, 12
Matzoh Dumplings for Golden Chicken Soup, 55
Meat Dumplings for Golden Chicken Soup, 57
Mexican Chicken, 73
Mexican Chicken Bake, 72
Mexican Chicken Roast, 74
Miami Chicken Salad, 112

N

Noodles for Golden Chicken Soup, 56

O

Old-Fashioned Stuffed Roast Chicken, 38
Orange-Stuffed Chicken, 41
Oriental Chicken
  Chicken and Almonds, Chinese Style, 132
  Chicken Chow Mein with Filberts, 131
  Chicken Curry, 122
  Chicken Korean Style, 124
  Chicken Legs, Oriental Style, 122
  Chicken with Cauliflower, Chinese Style, 129
  Chinese Chicken and Peppers, 130
  Chinese Chicken with Blanched Almonds, 128
  Chinese Chicken with Chestnuts, 135
  Chinese Chicken with Mushrooms and Scallions, 134
  Chinese Chicken with Pineapple, 128
  Chinese Style Chicken with Rice, 133
  Green Asparagus and White Chicken, Japanese Style, 125
  Hawaiian Flair Chicken, 127
  Korean Style Chicken, 123
  Japanese Chicken and Green Peas, 124
  Japanese Style Breast of Chicken #1, 126
  Japanese Style Chicken Breast #2, 126
Oriental chicken, secrets of making, 121
Oven Barbecued Broilers #1, 20
Oven Barbecued Broilers #3, 22
Oven-Fried Chicken #1, 16
Oven-Fried Chicken #2, 17
Oyster-Chicken Gumbo, 169

P

Parmesan-Romano Chicken Bake, 39
Peachy-Keen Chicken Roast, 46
Pilaff with Chicken Livers, 108
Pretzel Fried Chicken, 11
Puffy Squares for Golden Chicken Soup, 57

Q

Quick Chicken and Parsley Dumplings, 94
Quick Chicken and Vegetable Casserole, 99
Quick Chicken Casserole, 93
Quick Chicken in Wine, 95
Quick Chicken 'N Dumplings, 97
Quick Chicken Soufflé, 106
Quick Chinese Chicken, 101
Quickie Chicken and Rice, 102
Quick-to-make dishes
  Cheese Pinwheels and Chicken, 110
  Chicken and Broccoli Bake, 99
  Chicken and Chip Casserole, 104
  Chicken Croquettes, 98
  Chicken Gizzards with Herb Rice, 100
  Chicken Livers Smothered in Onions, 93
  Chicken 'N Peas, 105
  Chicken Patties and Celery Root, 108
  Creamed Chicken Supreme, 96
  Pilaff with Chicken Livers, 108
  Quick Chicken and Parsley Dumplings, 94
  Quick Chicken and Vegetable Casserole, 99
  Quick Chicken Casserole, 93
  Quick Chicken in Wine, 95
  Quick Chicken 'N Dumplings, 97
  Quick Chicken Soufflé, 106
  Quick Chinese Chicken, 101
  Quickie Chicken and Rice, 102
  Skillet Chicken 'N Gravy, 103

R

Roast Chicken in Brandy Sauce, 33
Roast Chicken in Foil, 33
Roast Chicken in Rhine Wine and Vodka, 46

Roast Chicken Supreme, 37
Roast Chicken with Gravy, 147
Roast Chicken with Pomegranate
  Stuffing, 40
Roast Chicken with Raisin Stuffing,
  45
Roast Chicken with Savory Rice
  Stuffing, 36
Roast Chicken with Toasted
  Almond Stuffing, 42
Roast Chicken with Vegetable
  Stuffing, 44
Roast Chicken with Water
  Chestnut Stuffing, 34
Roast Chicken with Wine, 43
Roasting chicken, 31
Rocambeau Chicken, 162
Rumanian Chicken Pancakes, 85

S

Salad making, 111
Salads
  Chicken-Almond Salad Bowl,
    119
  Chicken and Walnut Salad, 114
  Chicken-Olive Salad, 113
  Chicken, Peas and Cheese, 111
  Chicken Salad, 112
  Chicken Salad Supreme, 117
  Chicken Salad with Fruit, 113
  Chicken Salad with Hazelnuts,
    118
  Cranberry and Chicken Salad,
    114
  Dixie Chicken Salad, 115
  Freezer Tray Chicken Salad, 115
  French Bean and Chicken Salad,
    119
  Hot Chicken Salad #1, 116
  Hot Chicken Salad #2, 116
  Jellied Chicken Salad, 118
  Miami Chicken Salad, 112
  Sweet and Sour Chicken Salad,
    120
Sandwiches
  Chicken and Chives Sandwiches,
    67
  Chicken and Jellied Tongue
    Sandwiches, 66
  Chicken and Parmesan
    Sandwiches, 71
  Chicken and Walnut
    Sandwiches, 68
  Chicken Burgers Supreme, 62
  Chicken, Ham and Egg
    Sandwiches, 68
  Chicken Hash Patties in Buns,
    63
  Chicken Loaf for Rye Bread
    Sandwiches, 65
  Chicken Liver Sandwich
    Spread, 69
  Chicken 'N Cheese Burgers, 65

Hot Chicken and Veal Loaf
  Sandwiches, 64
Hot Chicken Sandwiches
  Supreme, 66
Jellied Chicken Loaf, 170
White Chicken Meat and Olive
  Sandwiches, 67
Sandwich making, 61–62
Sauced Southern Roast Chicken,
  146
Simple Barbecued Broilers, 20
Simple Fried Chicken, 18
Simple Oven Fried Chicken, 16
Skillet Chicken 'N Gravy, 103
Skillet Chicken Stew #1, 156
Skillet Chicken Stew #2, 157
Skillet Fried Chicken, 18
Soups
  Chicken Bone Soup from
    Roast Chicken Bones, 51
  Chicken Booyah, 58
  Chicken Broth, 48
  Chicken-Corn Chowder, 49
  Chicken Gumbo, 59
  Chicken-Vegetable Soup, 60
  Cream of Chicken Soup
    Supreme, 50
  Golden Chicken Soup—Jewish
    Style, 54
  Italian Egg and Chicken Broth,
    53
  Italian Style Chicken Soup, 52
Spanish Chicken, 76
Stewing Chicken, 47, 72, 111, 151
Stews
  Chicken a la King, 158
  Chicken and Celery Root Pot,
    159
  Chicken Pot Pie, 154
  Chicken Stewed in Cream—
    Oven Method, 152
  Chicken Stewed in Beer, 160
  Chicken Stewed with Mush-
    rooms—Oven Method, 153
  Skillet Chicken Stew #1, 156
  Skillet Chicken Stew #2, 157
Storing chicken, 9–10
Stuffed Chicken Breasts with
  Mushrooms, 170
Stuffing for chicken, 31–32
Sweet and Sour Chicken Salad, 120

T

Thawing frozen chicken, 10, 92
Tropical Chicken with Wine, 88
Turkish Chicken in Quince
  Shells, 90
Turkish Chicken with Sesame
  Seed, 90

W

White Chicken Meat and Olive
  Sandwiches, 67